**YOU
CANNOT
BE SERIOUS!**

YOU CANNOT BE SERIOUS!

THE GRAPHIC GUIDE TO TENNIS

MARK HODGKINSON

CONTENTS

THE RULES OF THE GAME

Do you know the dimensions of a tennis court? And the basic rules? Or some of the more unusual rules, such as what happens if a ball hits a bird during a rally? Or if, without striking any wildlife, the ball simply breaks in mid-air?

The basic rules

● The server hits the ball into the service box diagonally opposite, and from point to point alternates between serving from the deuce court and the advantage court. The server has two chances to land the ball into the court. If the ball touches the net and is in, a 'let' is called and the server is given another chance.

● The point is lost if the server makes two faults or if one of the players can't return the ball into their opponent's court before the ball bounces twice.

Scoring

● The score in games goes as follows: love, 15, 30, 40, game. If both players have won three points, the score is deuce, and whoever takes the next point has advantage. If the same player takes the next point, they win the game. Otherwise, it's back to deuce. You need to be two points ahead to win the game. The first to six games snaffles the set, but you must be two games clear, so you can't win 6–5, though you can take it 7–5.

● If you are playing a tie-break set, you play a tie-break at six games all, with the first to seven points, although you need to be at least two points clear.

● If you're playing an advantage set, you continue until one player is leading by two games.

● In professional tennis, matches are played as the best of three or of five sets.

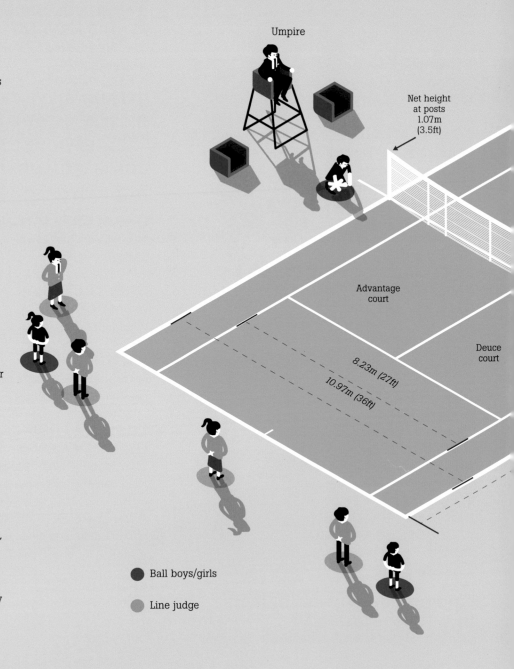

Umpire

Net height at posts 1.07m (3.5ft)

Advantage court

Deuce court

8.23m (27ft)

10.97m (36ft)

● Ball boys/girls

● Line judge

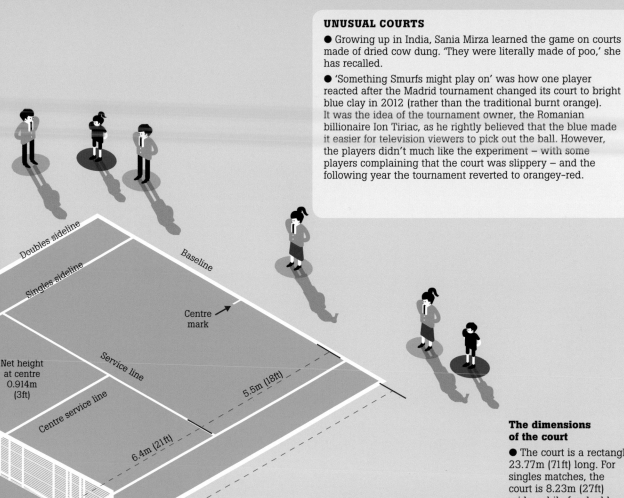

Doubles sideline

Singles sideline

Baseline

Centre mark

Net height at centre 0.914m (3ft)

Service line

Centre service line

5.5m (18ft)

6.4m (21ft)

23.77 m (71ft)

The dimensions of the court

● The court is a rectangle 23.77m (71ft) long. For singles matches, the court is 8.23m (27ft) wide, while for doubles matches, it is 10.97m (36ft) wide. The lines at the ends of the court are called baselines, while the lines on the sides are known as sidelines, with the areas between the singles sidelines and the doubles sidelines called the tramlines.

● The net should be attached to the posts at a height of 1.07m (3.5ft), while the height at the centre should be 0.914m (3ft).

● On either side of the court is a service line, which is 6.4m (21ft) from the net, and also parallel to the net.

● On both sides, the area between the net and the service line is divided into equal parts by the centre service line.

UNUSUAL RULES

● If the ball hits a bird flying over the court, the point should be replayed.

● If a ball breaks during a point, the point should be replayed, but if the ball has just gone soft, there shouldn't be a replay.

● At tournaments played at 1,219m (4,000ft) or higher, balls must be acclimatised for a minimum of 60 days at that same altitude.

ORIGINS OF THE SPORT

Debate continues over the origins of tennis. Can the sport be traced back to ancient Egypt or to 11th-century French monks? And who was the 'Welsh Renaissance Man'?

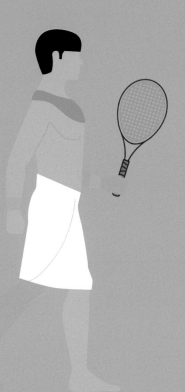

3500 BC

Some tennis historians think the sport originated in ancient Egypt, pointing to how the word 'racket' derives from the Arabic *rahat*, meaning 'palm of the hand'.

1100

But most historians believe it was French monks in the 11th or 12th century who first played a version of tennis – their game was known as '*jeu de paume*' or 'game of the palm'. The French influence can still be seen – for example, the name 'tennis' originates from the cries of 'Tenez!' or 'Take that!', which would be heard around the cloisters as the monks struck the ball. 'Deuce' comes from '*à deux le jeu*', which means 'to both in the game' or that the scores are level, while 'love' for zero is believed to derive from '*l'oeuf*', as an egg is a similar shape to the number.

1599

1874

1877

'Jeu de paume' grew into real or royal tennis, with the sport mentioned in William Shakespeare's *Henry V*, written around 1599, in which the young king is given tennis balls by the French Dauphin, a gift that supposedly mocked the recipient's youth. Henry VIII was a keen tennis player and had a court built at Hampton Court Palace (it is said he was playing tennis when he was informed of his wife Anne Boleyn's execution).

'A Welsh Renaissance Man' is how Major Walter Clopton Wingfield was once described – another way of thinking of him is as the inventor of modern tennis. For it was he, in 1874, who patented the game (with that patent signed by Queen Victoria), though the name he gave it – 'Sphairistike', which derives from the Greek for 'ball skills' – never caught on and it became known as 'lawn tennis'. In the words of one newspaper at the time: 'The monopoly of croquet is at last broken.'

Wimbledon, which was first played in 1877, is the oldest tennis tournament in the world. The US Open was first played in 1881, while the French Open began in 1891 and the Australian Open in 1905.

ICON **ROGER FEDERER**

As well as being the most urbane and elegant tennis player in the sport's history, Federer is also – and there is almost universal agreement on this – the greatest.

THE FACTS

NICKNAME

The Fed/GOAT
(Greatest Of All Time)

DATE OF BIRTH

8 August 1981

BIRTHPLACE

Basel, Switzerland

HEIGHT

1.85m (6ft 1in)

PLAYING STYLE

Right-handed (one-handed backhand)

20

The man with the most Grand Slam singles titles.

5

The only man in the Open era to win five successive US Open singles titles. Only the second man, after Björn Borg, to win five successive Wimbledon titles.

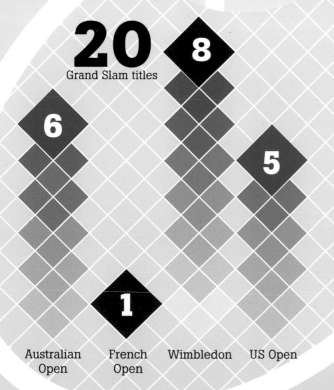

RECORDS

2009

The year Federer became the sixth man to achieve the Career Grand Slam (at the French Open). Rafael Nadal and Novak Djokovic have since joined him in that club.

8

His record-breaking number of Wimbledon titles.

65

Federer holds the record for consecutive majors played – the 2016 French Open was the first Slam he missed this century.

23

The record number of consecutive Grand Slam semi-final appearances.

10

A record for consecutive Grand Slam finals.

20 Grand Slam titles

6

8

5

1

Australian Open | French Open | Wimbledon | US Open

FEDERER
IN NUMBERS

302

The record number of weeks Federer has spent as the world number one.

237

The record number of consecutive weeks Federer has spent at the top of the tennis rankings.

1,000

In 2015, Federer became the third man in history to win more than 1,000 matches. Jimmy Connors and Ivan Lendl were the first two to reach four figures.

2008

The year that Federer won an Olympic gold medal – in the doubles competition with Stan Wawrinka.

2014

The year that Switzerland won the Davis Cup for the first time, with Federer completing the victory against France in the final.

6

Federer was the first man to score six titles at the ATP Finals (the season-ending tournament).

64 million

Federer's income in US dollars in 2017, according to an estimate by *Forbes* magazine, of which around 58 million came from endorsements and appearance fees.

95.3

Federer's winning percentage in 2005, the year in which he was at his most dominant – he won 81 matches and lost just four.

PRODIGIES

While tennis doesn't produce as many prodigies as it once did, the history books are full of over-achieving teenagers.

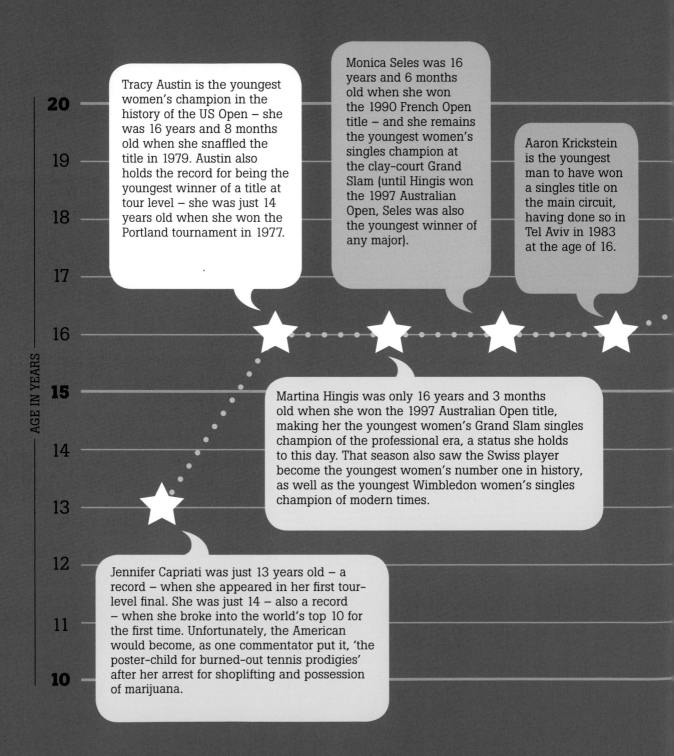

AGE IN YEARS

Tracy Austin is the youngest women's champion in the history of the US Open – she was 16 years and 8 months old when she snaffled the title in 1979. Austin also holds the record for being the youngest winner of a title at tour level – she was just 14 years old when she won the Portland tournament in 1977.

Monica Seles was 16 years and 6 months old when she won the 1990 French Open title – and she remains the youngest women's singles champion at the clay-court Grand Slam (until Hingis won the 1997 Australian Open, Seles was also the youngest winner of any major).

Aaron Krickstein is the youngest man to have won a singles title on the main circuit, having done so in Tel Aviv in 1983 at the age of 16.

Martina Hingis was only 16 years and 3 months old when she won the 1997 Australian Open title, making her the youngest women's Grand Slam singles champion of the professional era, a status she holds to this day. That season also saw the Swiss player become the youngest women's number one in history, as well as the youngest Wimbledon women's singles champion of modern times.

Jennifer Capriati was just 13 years old – a record – when she appeared in her first tour-level final. She was just 14 – also a record – when she broke into the world's top 10 for the first time. Unfortunately, the American would become, as one commentator put it, 'the poster-child for burned-out tennis prodigies' after her arrest for shoplifting and possession of marijuana.

'People looked at me as if I was from another planet,' Boris Becker observed after his victory at the 1985 Wimbledon Championships when he was 17 years and 7 months old. He remains the youngest men's singles champion in the tournament's history. Just to prove it hadn't been a fluke, he won again the following year, and then for a third occasion in 1989.

Just days after turning 19, Pete Sampras won the 1990 US Open title to become the youngest men's champion in the tournament's history. No one has beaten that record since.

Lleyton Hewitt is the youngest men's world number one in history – he was just 20 years old when he achieved that ranking.

Mats Wilander is the youngest Australian Open men's champion of the Open era – he was 19 years old when he won the title in 1983.

Michael Chang was 17 years and 3 months old when he won the 1989 French Open title to become the youngest men's Grand Slam singles champion in history. That's a record he still holds to this day, with his run in Paris largely remembered for the impudent, underarm serve he hit in his fourth-round match against Ivan Lendl (it's sometimes forgotten that he beat Stefan Edberg in the final).

Across both the amateur and professional eras, the youngest male winner of the Australian Open was Ken Rosewall – just 18 when he lifted the trophy in 1953. Remarkably, Rosewall also holds the record for being the oldest ever Grand Slam champion, winning the 1972 Australian Open at 37.

STYLES OF PLAY

Some might suggest that tennis has become homogenised, that everyone plays the same way – but they would be wrong. There are still a variety of different styles of play. If you're an aspiring amateur, here is how you need to play in each style and the champions to emulate.

THE BASELINE BASHER

This is how most (but certainly not all) modern professionals play tennis: by biffing the ball extremely hard from the back of the court. It's an exaggeration to say that the baseline bashers will only come to the net for the coin-toss and the handshake, but it's true that their trips into the service box will be rare.

What you'll need: Muscle in your forehand, and preferably in your backhand, too. A Plan B might be helpful, too – if your opponent is hitting the ball even harder and truer from the baseline, what are you going to do then?

Players to aspire to: Serena Williams, Rafael Nadal, Maria Sharapova.

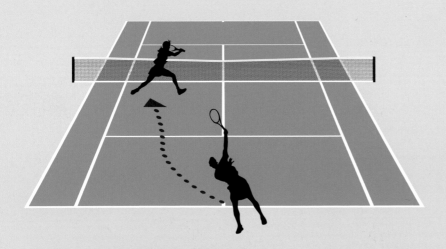

THE SERVE-AND-VOLLEYER

Like corduroy, beige and flared trousers, serve-and-volleying was big in the 1970s but has since fallen out of fashion. Over the decades, advances in racket technology have enabled returners to wallop the ball with explosive power, and that's why most servers now tend to stay back. But, for those bold enough to rush to the net behind their serve, this can be a rewarding style, especially as your opponent won't be used to it. Of this you can be sure: it won't be dull.

What you'll need: A decent serve, an even better volley and an appetite for risk.

Players to aspire to: Pete Sampras, John McEnroe, Martina Navratilova, Boris Becker.

THE COUNTER-PUNCHER

Respect the hustle. You'll find a counter-puncher on the baseline – or probably a few feet behind it – where they'll be absorbing an opponent's pressure, scrambling and defending. But they'll be waiting for the chance to strike, and in that moment will quickly switch from passive to aggressive as they go for a winner.

What you'll need: Consistency of shot, patience and at least one big weapon (probably your forehand).

Players to aspire to: Lleyton Hewitt, Andy Murray.

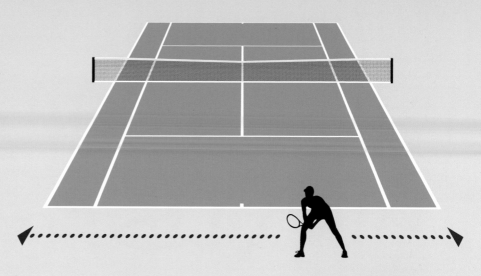

ALL-COURT PLAYER

Some players have all the skills, and look comfortable in every part of the court, and they can mix up their games, depending on the surface, the conditions and the opponent.

What you'll need: Lots of talent.

Players to aspire to: Roger Federer, Agnieszka Radwanska.

THE MOONBALLER

Perhaps the most frustrating of all adversaries on a tennis court is the player who keeps on looping the ball high into the air, and deep to the opponent's baseline – topspin forehand after topspin forehand. It's a style devoid of much art or guile. In truth, it's a style devoid of style. But there's no escaping the fact that it can be devilishly effective.

What you'll need: Solid groundstrokes, a high boredom threshold and a thick skin.

Player to aspire to: Conchita Martínez.

TENNIS LINGO

Bewildered by some of the language used in tennis? Drop these words into the conversation and you'll soon sound like a seasoned pro.

the tramlines

ALLEY

a 6–1 set (this is a carb-heavy sport, with a 6–0 set known as a 'bagel')

BREADSTICK

PULP

30-all, as in not quite deuce

the Greatest Of All Time

GOAT

Andre Agassi's name for clay-courters, also known as 'dirtballers'

high, slow groundstrokes, hit with lots of topspin

MOONBALL

DIRT-RAT

WHIFF

hitting an opponent with a ball struck at speed (usually deliberate, and a shot that Ivan Lendl took great delight in playing)

TAG

to completely miss the ball

GOLDEN SET

winning a set without losing a single point

HOT-DOG

also known as a 'tweener', this is a shot played when you have your back to the court and you strike the ball straight through your legs

HAIL MARY

a defensive lob

a shot hit with little pace and no spin, usually in a long rally to throw an opponent off their rhythm

JUNK BALL

SABR

Sneak Attack by Roger, a shot devised by Federer, who dashed forward to play his return from around the service line before continuing into the net

deliberately losing a match, or a set

TANK

THE EVOLUTION OF THE TENNIS RACKET

To make a tennis racket, you used to have to chop down a tree. Now the frames are made from innovative, futuristic materials you might find on a NASA mission, and along with synthetic, modern strings, those advances have enabled players to hit the ball with ever greater power and spin. But there are limits to how far you can take technology, with restrictions on the dimensions, and a list of other banned features.

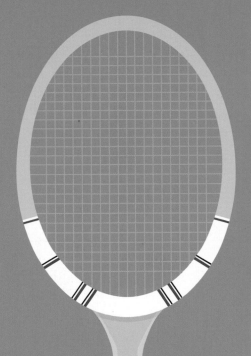

Material in the frame
The most common woods used were ash and maple.

Weight
Approximately 400g (14oz)

Head size
Around 420cm² (65 sq in)

Strings
Animal gut

Storage
If you didn't keep the racket in a head-press between matches, it would warp.

WOODEN

20

POWER OR CONTROL?

- A higher string tension will give a player more control, while a lower tension allows for greater power.
- A larger racket head will give a player more power and a bigger sweet spot, while a smaller head brings additional control.
- A heavier racket will add power to a player's shots, although it might prove tiring and cumbersome to swing.

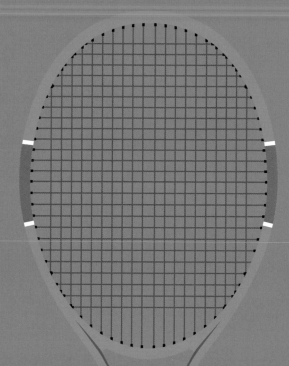

Material in the frame
Graphite, sometimes combined with Kevlar, fibreglass and titanium

Weight
Approximately 300g (10.5oz)

Strings
Nylon, although some professionals like a combination of synthetic and animal gut

Head size
Around 548–871cm² (85–135 sq in)

Storage
No need for a head-press

BANNED

- Your racket can't be longer than 73.7cm (29in).
- It mustn't be wider than 31.7cm (12.5in).
- A vibration-damping device is permitted, but it has to be outside the crossed string pattern.
- You mustn't have a battery or a solar cell on the racket that changes its playing characteristics.
- Your racket mustn't have double strings (which generate extreme amounts of spin).

MODERN

THE AUSTRALIAN OPEN IN NUMBERS

It was Roger Federer who first called the Australian Open 'The Happy Slam'. But it's also the major where players can become so overheated on court that there's a real danger of hallucination – one player thought he saw Snoopy, the cartoon dog.

40°

The temperature, in Celsius, at which the tournament's Extreme Heat Policy can be enacted, leading to the suspension of matches. However, for the policy to come into play, the Wet Bulb Globe Temperature – a combination of humidity, wind and temperature – must have reached 32.5°C or higher.

6

The number of games that Marcelo Ríos won in the 1998 men's singles final against Petr Korda, attracting accusations that he hadn't tried his best.

50°

On-court temperatures at the 2007 tournament approached 50°C.

212

Mark Edmondson's ranking the year he won the 1976 men's singles title. Just weeks earlier, he had been working as a hospital porter, cleaning windows and polishing floors. No one has ever scored a Grand Slam singles title with a lower ranking, while Edmondson also remains the last Australian man to have won the title.

4

The number of consecutive days during the 2014 Australian Open that the temperature exceeded 40°C, during Melbourne's longest heatwave for a century. Players' shoes and water bottles started to melt, but the greatest danger was to the competitors themselves, although the tournament's chief medical officer didn't seem overly concerned: 'We evolved on the high plains of Africa chasing antelope for eight hours under these conditions.'

The number of hallucinating tennis players who became so overheated during the 2014 Australian Open that they thought they had visions of a cartoon dog. That player was Canada's **Frank Dancevic**: 'I was dizzy from the middle of the first set and then I saw Snoopy and I thought, "Wow, Snoopy, that's weird".'

The year that the tournament was first played, making it the youngest of the four Grand Slams.

1905
1986
2008

728,763

The record for the highest Grand Slam event attendance, which was achieved during the 2017 Australian Open.

The year that the Australian Open wasn't played, thanks to a calendar change from December to January (so there were tournaments in December 1985 and January 1987).

The year that the tournament last changed surfaces, to Plexicushion, a type of hard court. Originally played on grass, it switched to hard courts and then Rebound Ace, in 1988, which was used for 20 years.

The number of spectators who were thrown out of the 2007 tournament for fighting. Just a couple of days after Federer had called this 'The Happy Slam', the Australian Open saw the first riot in the history of the majors.

40

Before the invention of the jet engine, this was approximately how many days it would take players to travel by boat from Europe to Australia. Understandably, only a small number of Europeans made the trip to the tournament.

7

The number of cities to have hosted the tournament. Five of those host cities have been Australian – Melbourne, Sydney, Adelaide, Perth and Brisbane – while it has also been played in Christchurch and Hastings, both in New Zealand.

ICON SERENA WILLIAMS

The greatest female tennis player of all time? Almost certainly. There's also an argument to suggest Williams is simply the greatest of all players.

THE FACTS

NICKNAME
Meka

DATE OF BIRTH
26 September 1981

BIRTHPLACE
Saginaw, United States

HEIGHT
1.75m (5ft 9in)

PLAYING STYLE
Right-handed (two-handed backhand)

2

Twice she has accomplished the 'Serena Slam' by holding all four majors simultaneously, across the 2002–03 and 2014-15 seasons.

RECORDS

23
Williams has won more Grand Slam singles titles in the Open era than any other player, man or woman.

35
Serena's age when she became the oldest world number one in history.

7
More Australian Open titles in the Open era than any other woman.

84
More prize money, in millions of US dollars (figure correct at end of 2017), than any female tennis player in history.

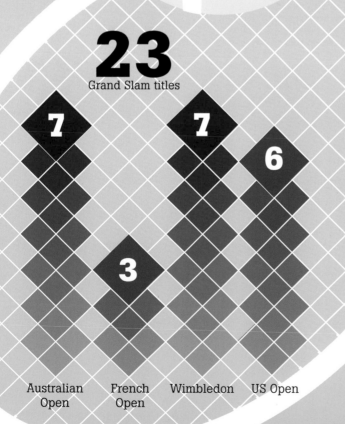

23
Grand Slam titles

7 Australian Open
3 French Open
7 Wimbledon
6 US Open

WILLIAMS
IN NUMBERS

2
Williams was two months pregnant when she won the 2017 Australian Open.

4
She has won Grand Slam titles under four presidents of the United States – Bill Clinton, George W. Bush, Barack Obama and Donald Trump.

2014
The year that Williams had her first show at New York Fashion Week, showcasing her range of clothes.

14
Williams' absence, in years, from the tournament at the Indian Wells Tennis Garden after a 2001 incident when 'ugliness rained down on me, hard'. One of the chapters in her autobiography is entitled, 'The Fiery Darts of Indian Wells', in which she wrote of a 'genteel lynch mob'. In 2015, she forgave the crowd and returned to the tournament.

TRAINING METHODS

From egg-shaped chambers to pole dancing, from magic mountains to medieval torture devices, tennis players have found all sorts of ways to stay in shape.

Thomas Muster must be the only leading player in history to have practised his forehand while sitting on a chair with his leg in a cast. Eager to return to the training court after being hit by a drunk driver, Muster had a chair specially made so he could swing away from a seated position.

Anyone hiking through the Swiss mountains in 2016 would have stood a fair chance of bumping into **Roger Federer**. With the Swiss player missing the second half of the season as he recovered from a knee operation, he built up his fitness by hiking through the mountains. Those walks would have been much quieter than some of Federer's other work-outs – he has been known to listen to heavy metal, with the volume turned up high, when lifting weights in the gym.

'Magic Mountain' is the name that **Andre Agassi** gave to the hill in Nevada that he used to sprint up. 'Andre's lungs were screaming,' his fitness trainer Gil Reyes said.

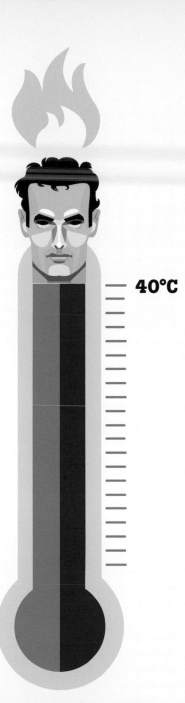

40°C

Novak Djokovic's physical prowess can be attributed partly to an egg, or, more precisely, to sitting inside an egg-shaped pressure chamber that simulates high altitude. 'It's like a spaceship – it's very interesting technology,' he has said.

Over the course of his career, **Andy Murray** has endured extreme temperatures – intense heat and icy cold. The extreme heat was in the Bikram yoga studio, which is 40°C or warmer. 'Until you do it, you can't comment on how difficult it is. It's tough, it's ugly,' Murray has said. After a long match or training session, Murray will sit in an ice bath, with the cold water helping to drain the lactic acid from his muscles. He has also been known to use a Gyrotonic machine, which incorporates pulleys, levers and weights, and has been described as 'a mix of yoga and ballet, enacted on a medieval torture device'.

Pole dancing is 'an incredible workout', according to **Serena Williams**, who has also been known to work on her fitness by performing contemporary dance routines. As children, Williams and her older sister, Venus, used to throw American footballs around, as their father Richard believed it would strengthen the muscles they needed for their serves.

HAWK-EYE

When Hawk-Eye was introduced to tennis just over 10 years ago, the worry was that the line-calling technology might take some of the theatre out of the sport. How could you expect the modern generation to bring you McEnroe-style emotion when you don't even give them a bad call to rage against? But, as it turned out, Hawk-Eye has added to the spectacle, especially when used on break points, set points and match points.

2005

The International Tennis Federation approved Hawk-Eye for professional use.

2006

Miami was the first tour-level event to have Hawk-Eye. The US Open was the first Grand Slam to use it.

2007

The Australian Open and Wimbledon became the second and third majors to use Hawk-Eye.

80

Hawk-Eye Innovations has said that more than 80 events are using its line-calling technology.

3.66

The average Hawk-Eye error, in millimetres, which is about the same length as the fluff on the ball.

CORRECT CHALLENGES

AUSTRALIAN OPEN

MEN	**30.4%**
WOMEN	**26.8%**

OVERALL AT THE GRAND SLAMS

MEN	**28%**
WOMEN	**27%**

WIMBLEDON

MEN	**29.8%**
WOMEN	**29.5%**

French Open

The French Open doesn't use Hawk-Eye, preferring to have the umpire step down from their chair to inspect a mark on the clay.

US OPEN

MEN	**24%**
WOMEN	**24.7%**

THE MATCH THAT PROBABLY CONVINCED TENNIS TO TURN TO HAWK-EYE

Serena Williams' quarter-final defeat to fellow American Jennifer Capriati at the 2004 US Open is remembered for a number of questionable line calls, although Williams was, of course, unable to query any of them because Hawk-Eye wasn't in place. John McEnroe, who was commentating on the match, said: 'Hawk-Eye, please – this is getting ridiculous.'

SOME PLAYERS STILL AREN'T COMPLETELY HAPPY

Roger Federer has his reservations about Hawk-Eye. 'What I struggle with is I don't think it's 100 per cent accurate. Let's say 99 per cent, fine. It's still not 100 per cent in my opinion. I still see calls I don't quite understand. But I still think it's fine to have it.'

• Other players would like to see Hawk-Eye used on all courts at the biggest tournaments, and not just on the show courts. But such a move would come with a heavy cost, as the technology isn't cheap to install and maintain.

TIMELINE OF GREATEST FEMALE PLAYERS

Here is a chart of the most successful female players of modern times – Serena Williams, Steffi Graf, Chris Evert and Martina Navratilova – following their careers from when they each scored their first Grand Slam singles title.

TOTAL MAJORS AT YEAR-END

- Chris Evert
- Martina Navratilova
- Steffi Graf

Serena Williams

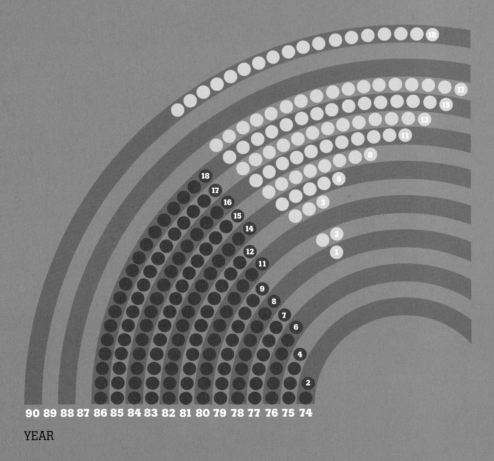

YEAR

90 89 88 87 86 85 84 83 82 81 80 79 78 77 76 75 74

85 86 87 88 89 90 91 92 93 94 95 96 97 98 99 00 01 02 03 04 05 06 07 08 09 10 11 12 13 14 15 16 17

YEAR

JUNIOR AND SENIOR GRAND SLAM CHAMPIONS

A small number of players have won the junior singles title at a Grand Slam and then gone all the way to senior singles glory at the same tournament. Here they are – including only those players who won at least one senior title in the Open era, which started in 1968.

Girls' titles   Women's titles   Boys' titles   Men's titles

1 = years between junior and first senior title

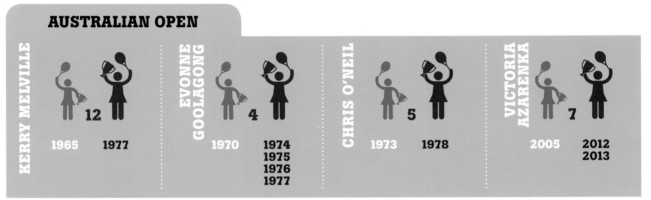

AUSTRALIAN OPEN

KERRY MELVILLE — 12 — 1965 — 1977

EVONNE GOOLAGONG — 4 — 1970 — 1974 1975 1976 1977

CHRIS O'NEIL — 5 — 1973 — 1978

VICTORIA AZARENKA — 7 — 2005 — 2012 2013

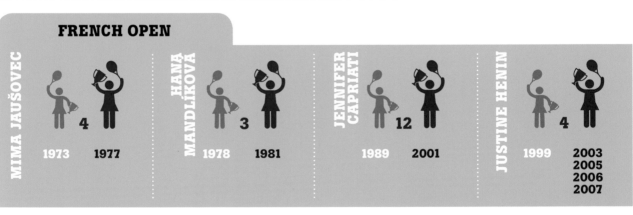

FRENCH OPEN

MIMA JAUŠOVEC — 4 — 1973 — 1977

HANA MANDLÍKOVÁ — 3 — 1978 — 1981

JENNIFER CAPRIATI — 12 — 1989 — 2001

JUSTINE HENIN — 4 — 1999 — 2003 2005 2006 2007

WIMBLEDON

MARTINA HINGIS — 3 — 1994 — 1997

AMÉLIE MAURESMO — 10 — 1996 — 2006

US OPEN

LINDSAY DAVENPORT — 6 — 1992 — 1998

AUSTRALIAN OPEN

KEN ROSEWALL
3
1950 | 1953
1955
1971
1972

ROD LAVER
3
1957 | 1960
1962
1969

JOHN NEWCOMBE
12
1961 | 1973
1962 | 1975
1963

STEFAN EDBERG
2
1983 | 1985
1975

FRENCH OPEN

KEN ROSEWALL
1
1952 | 1953
1968

IVAN LENDL
6
1978 | 1984
1986
1987

MATS WILANDER
1
1981 | 1982
1985
1988

STAN WAWRINKA
12
2003 | 2015

WIMBLEDON

BJÖRN BORG
4
1972 | 1976–80

PAT CASH
5
1982 | 1987

STEFAN EDBERG
5
1983 | 1988
1990

ROGER FEDERER
5
1998 | 2003–7
2009
2012
2017

US OPEN

STEFAN EDBERG
8
1983 | 1991
1992

ANDY RODDICK
3
2000 | 2003

ANDY MURRAY
8
2004 | 2012

CELEBRATION TIME

Winning a tournament, or even a single point, brings a feeling of euphoria – it also brings the opportunity to show some personality.

Radek Štěpánek
The Czech is known for 'The Worm', a breakdancing routine he picked up while drinking Schnapps at an Alpine ski resort.

Andrew Ilie
Tennis once had its own Incredible Hulk – Ilie, an Australian who would mark his most important victories by ripping his shirt to pieces.

Novak Djokovic
The Serbian has celebrated winning Wimbledon by grazing on the Centre Court grass, which he has said 'tastes very, very good'.

Michaël Llodra
After winning the 2004 Australian Open doubles title, Llodra and his partner, Arnaud Clément, stripped down to their underwear before throwing all their clothes into the crowd. Llodra then emptied the spare clothes in his bag and also tossed those into the stands.

Gustavo Kuerten
His love for Roland Garros was such that he liked to draw a heart in the clay and then lie down inside it.

Mikhail Youzhny
The son of a Soviet army colonel, Youzhny is known for his military-style salutes. He salutes with his right hand and puts a racket on his head with his left.

Jim Courier
Just hours after a Melbourne newspaper disclosed that the River Yarra contained high levels of contamination, Courier jumped into the dirty water to celebrate winning the 1992 Australian Open. The next year, he did the same again.

Andy Murray

To mark a comeback win at Wimbledon in 2008, which had been a test of his new physical endurance, Murray rolled up his sleeve and flexed his bicep Popeye-style. There has been greater mystery over a celebration that Murray used for years – tilting his head back and looking at the sky. He was reluctant to disclose the significance.

Andy Murray

After winning his first ATP title, in San Jose in 2006, a teenage Andy Murray climbed into the stands to kiss his girlfriend and future wife, Kim Sears. Unfortunately for Sears, the moment was captured by photographers, shown in British newspapers and seen by her teachers. She was supposed to have been in school.

Maria Sharapova

When the Russian dropped the US Open trophy after winning the 2006 title her phone immediately started buzzing. 'All my friends texted me saying, "Typical Maria". Things like that always happen to me. I'm a goofball. I'm the dork of the group.'

Rafael Nadal

Nadal's dentist can't be too happy about his client's habit of biting every trophy he wins.

Lleyton Hewitt

If the Australian wasn't pumping his fist in the manner of someone starting a lawnmower or yelling 'C'mon', he was doing 'The Vicht' salute. This has been described as bending your hand into a shadow-puppet duck and pointing it at your forehead. While it was Swedish players, including multiple Grand Slam champion Mats Wilander, who introduced this salute, it became a signature Hewitt celebration.

Bob and Mike Bryan

The brothers' mid-air chest bumps are harder to do than they look. 'I played with Venus Williams in the mixed doubles and once after winning a point she came flying in to do a chest bump,' Bob has recalled. 'I was quite scared.'

Rafael Nadal

To celebrate his first Wimbledon victory, in 2008, Nadal climbed up into Centre Court and then over the roof of the TV commentary boxes to reach the Royal Box and say hello to the Crown Prince of Spain. Rafa was continuing a tradition started by Pat Cash in 1987, who was the first to scramble into the stadium after Wimbledon victory.

Roger Federer and Stan Wawrinka

The Swiss players performed their 'Campfire Routine' after winning doubles gold at the 2008 Beijing Olympics. With Wawrinka lying on the ground, Federer pretended to toast his hands over his partner as if he were on fire.

Petr Korda

The Czech did cartwheels and his signature scissor-kicks after winning the 1998 Australian Open.

ICON RAFAEL NADAL

Into double figures for French Open titles, Nadal is the King of Roland Garros and the greatest clay-court player of all time. He is also a force on hard and grass courts.

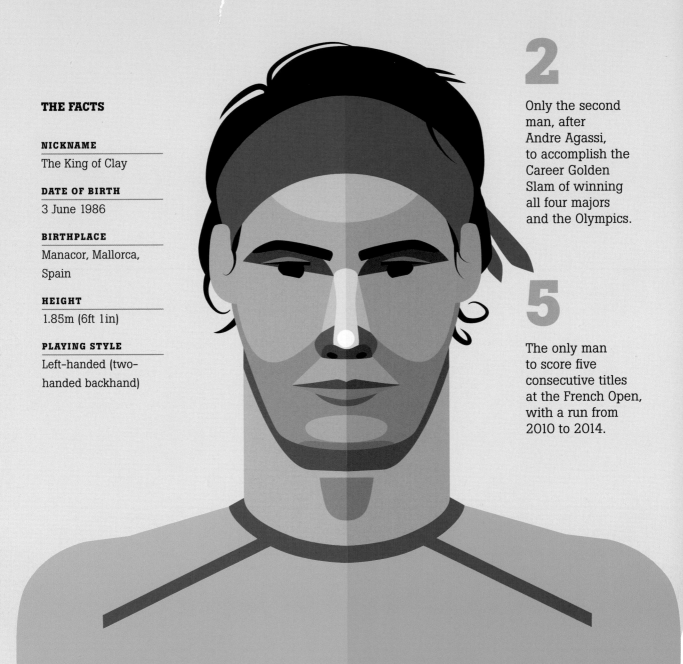

THE FACTS

NICKNAME
The King of Clay

DATE OF BIRTH
3 June 1986

BIRTHPLACE
Manacor, Mallorca, Spain

HEIGHT
1.85m (6ft 1in)

PLAYING STYLE
Left-handed (two-handed backhand)

2

Only the second man, after Andre Agassi, to accomplish the Career Golden Slam of winning all four majors and the Olympics.

5

The only man to score five consecutive titles at the French Open, with a run from 2010 to 2014.

RECORDS
10
With 'La Decima' at the 2017 French Open, Nadal became the first player of either sex to win the same Grand Slam tournament ten times.

81
The longest single-surface streak in men's tennis history, with 81 consecutive match victories on clay from April 2005 to May 2007.

31
Nadal was 31 years old when in 2017 he became the oldest ever season-ending number one.

10

16
Grand Slam titles

1
Australian Open

2
French Open

3
Wimbledon

US Open

10
Nadal is the first Open-era player to win three tournaments 10 times. In 2017 he took his 10th Monte Carlo title, as well as hitting double figures in Barcelona and at the French Open

0
The number of rackets Nadal has broken, or even thrown, during his professional career.

6
The number of Nadal's fears – the dark, thunderstorms, dogs, the sea, spiders and flying. 'I really hate the dark. I'm scared when it gets dark. Sometimes I need to sleep with the TV on.'

10
For 10 consecutive years, Nadal won at least one Grand Slam singles title, with a run from 2005 to 2014.

31
The number of consecutive matches that Nadal had won at the French Open before he lost at Roland Garros for the first time in his career, with defeat to Robin Söderling in the fourth round of the 2009 tournament.

THE RICH LIST

Such is Roger Federer's wealth that he might one day make it on to the *Forbes* billionaires list, and he's not the only tennis player who has grown rich from the sport. Federer wasn't even the first to win more than US$100 million in prize money.

KEY (US$ million)
- ■ Prize money
- □ Endorsements and appearance fees

• The highest-earning tennis players, according to a list published by *Forbes* magazine in 2017.

NOVAK DJOKOVIC
$37.6
■ $9.6
□ $28

2

Novak Djokovic was the first man to win more than $100 million in career prize money, which he accomplished at the 2016 French Open.

7

STAN WAWRINKA
$19.2
■ $7.2
□ $12

ANGELIQUE KERBER
$12.6
■ $7.6
□ $5

8

9

MILOS RAONIC
$11.8
■ $4.8
□ $7

10

VENUS WILLIAMS
$10.5
■ $3.5
□ $7

1 ROGER FEDERER
$64
- $6
- $58

3 KEI NISHIKORI
$33.9
- $3.9
- $30

4 RAFAEL NADAL
$31.5
- $5.5
- $26

5 ANDY MURRAY
$28.8
- $14.8
- $14

6 SERENA WILLIAMS
$27
- $8
- $19

Serena Williams leads the all-time prize money list for women's tennis by tens of millions of dollars – she has earned more than $80 million, which is more than double the second-placed woman, Maria Sharapova.

BIGGEST ENDORSEMENT CONTRACTS AND APPEARANCE FEES

Roger Federer's 10-year contract with Nike has been valued at $120 million, paying $12 million a year.

Maria Sharapova's 8-year deal with Nike has been valued at $70 million, paying $8.5 million a year.

Rafael Nadal's 5-year contract with Nike has been valued at $50 million, paying $10 million a year.

Kei Nishikori's 5-year deal with Uniqlo has been valued at $50 million, paying $10 million a year.

EXHIBITIONS

Federer is believed to earn up to $2 million for playing an exhibition match.

INCREASE IN WIMBLEDON PRIZE MONEY

1968 The men's singles champion at the first Wimbledon of the Open era received £2,000, while the women's champion received £750.

2017 The men's and women's singles champions each received £2.2 million.

INCREASE IN US OPEN PRIZE MONEY

1968 The men's singles champion won $14,000 and the women's singles champion $6,000.

2017 The men's and women's singles champions each received $3.7 million.

SPIN MASTERS

Which players generate the most spin with their forehands and backhands? These figures are based on analysis by John Yandell, a tennis researcher and videographer.

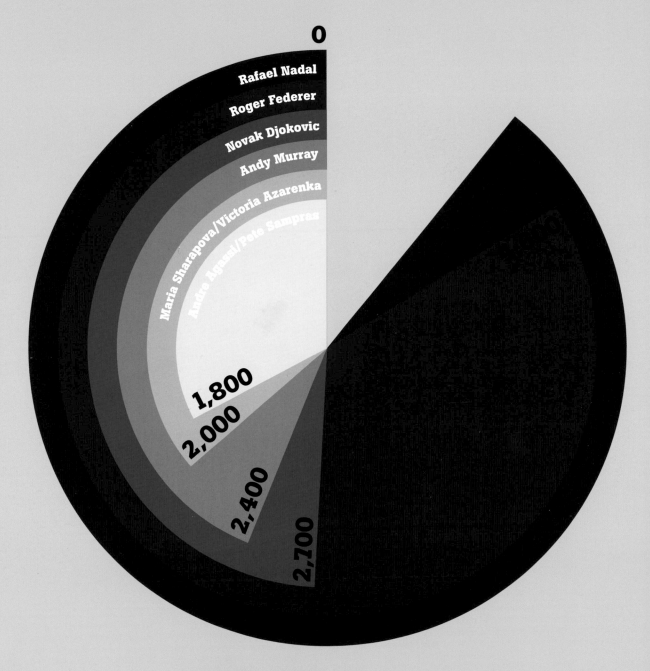

0

Rafael Nadal

Roger Federer

Novak Djokovic

Andy Murray

Maria Sharapova/Victoria Azarenka

Andre Agassi/Pete Sampras

1,800

2,000

2,400

2,700

Forehand – maximum revolutions per minute

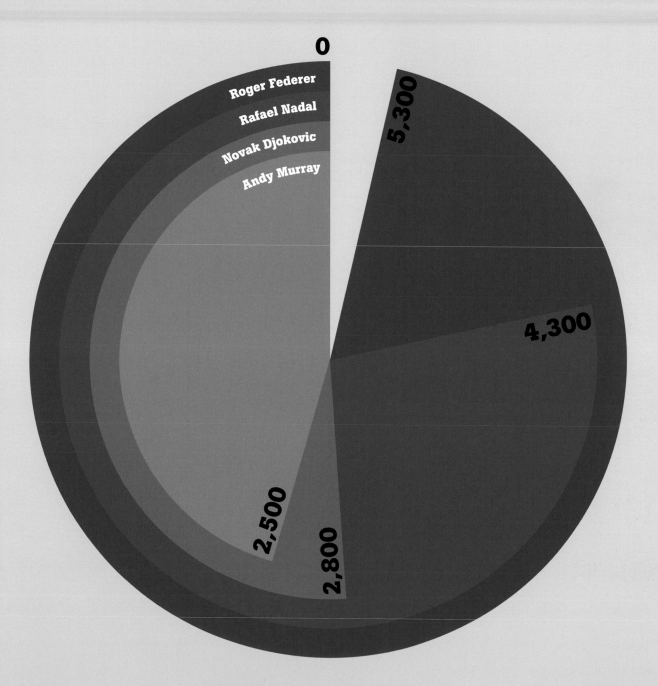

Backhand – maximum revolutions per minute

THE SHORTEST SHORTS

In the 1970s and 1980s, men's tennis shorts were so small they bordered on the indecent. But exactly how skimpy are we talking? For comparison, here are the lengths of players' shorts worn at Wimbledon from that era, and also the measurements of modern players' shorts, all based on displays at the Wimbledon Lawn Tennis Museum.

40cm

33cm

32.5cm

Pete Sampras
The Wimbledon Museum's curators believe that the American, who won seven titles between 1993 and 2000, had possibly tailored his shorts to make them shorter.

Jimmy Connors
Connors, who scored two Wimbledon titles in 1974 and 1982, has the second smallest shorts in the museum's collection.

Björn Borg
It's difficult to know how he moved in shorts that tiny, but despite the fashion choice, Borg won five successive Wimbledon titles from 1976 to 1980.

1933
Bunny Austin became the first player to wear shorts at Wimbledon ('I found sweat-sodden flannel trousers were weighing me down, so my tailor ran up some prototype shorts').

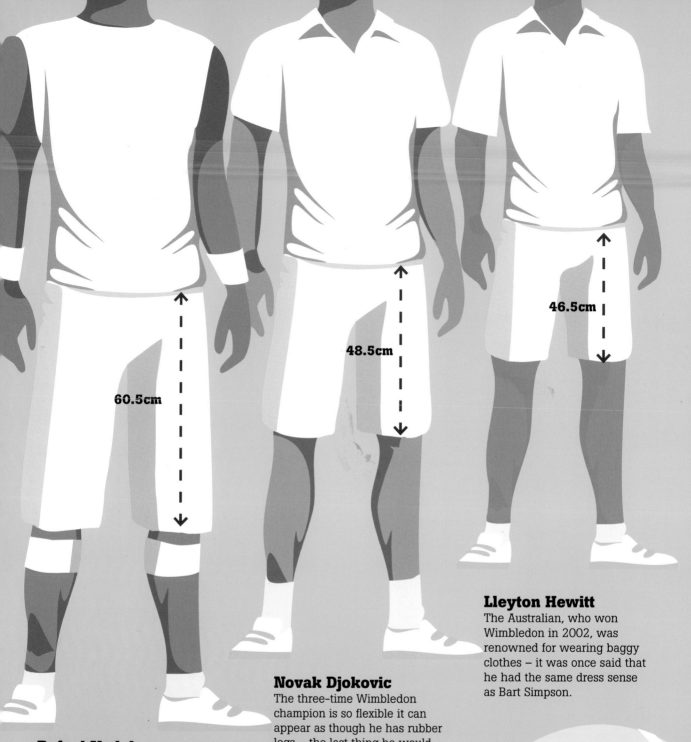

60.5cm

48.5cm

46.5cm

Lleyton Hewitt
The Australian, who won Wimbledon in 2002, was renowned for wearing baggy clothes – it was once said that he had the same dress sense as Bart Simpson.

Novak Djokovic
The three-time Wimbledon champion is so flexible it can appear as though he has rubber legs – the last thing he would have wanted was to have been constrained in a pair of shorts that were too tight.

Rafael Nadal
When the Spaniard won his first title at Wimbledon, beating Roger Federer in the epic 2008 final, he was wearing a pair of three-quarter-length capri pants that made him look as though he had just stepped off a Mallorcan beach.

1947
American Jack Kramer became the first man to win the Wimbledon singles title in shorts. But it wasn't until 2013, the year of Andy Murray's first victory, that a Briton won Wimbledon in shorts.

OLYMPICS . . . IN NUMBERS

The inclusion of tennis in the Olympics has been controversial, with some believing it shouldn't be an Olympic sport when a gold medal falls some way below a Grand Slam as the peak of a player's career. For all that, the elite truly care about standing at the top of the podium.

0

The number of pairs of tennis shoes, or pairs of flannel trousers, or rackets, that John Boland, an Irish student, brought to Athens in 1896. Boland was on holiday and hadn't intended to compete in the tennis tournament at the inaugural modern Olympics. But, having been persuaded to take part, he found some trousers, 'a tennis bat of sorts' and some shoes with leather soles and heels, and won both the singles and doubles titles.

5

Venus Williams won her fifth Olympic medal at the 2016 Rio de Janeiro Olympics with a silver in the mixed doubles with Rajeev Ram. Her other medals – one for singles and three for women's doubles, alongside her sister, Serena – are all gold. Serena has four gold medals, one of which was won in women's singles.

64

Tennis' absence, in years, from the Olympics programme. Tennis was an Olympic sport from the inaugural 1896 Games until the 1924 Games. It didn't return until 1988.

1,500

The men's champion at the 1900 Olympics received 1,500 French Francs and a coffee-and-liqueurs table.

2

The number of Olympic tennis tournaments played in London in 1908 – the first was indoors at Queen's Club and the second outdoors on the Wimbledon grass.

1

Andy Murray is the only player to have won consecutive single titles, after his triumphs in London in 2012 and Rio de Janeiro in 2016.

12

The time, in years, between Richard Williams surviving the sinking of RMS *Titanic* in 1912 and winning the Olympic mixed doubles title at Paris in 1924.

1

With her victory in the women's singles event at the 2016 Rio de Janeiro Olympics, Monica Puig became the first man or woman representing Puerto Rico to win a gold medal.

2012

Roger Federer's best singles result at the Olympics came at the 2012 Games in London, when he was a silver medallist. It is the only major singles title that Federer hasn't won.

2

Chile had never won a gold medal at the Olympics, and then two came in quick succession at the 2004 Athens Games, with Nicolas Massu and Fernando Gonzalez winning the men's doubles competition, and Massu then taking the singles event.

PLAYERS IN TEARS

Whether you win or lose, playing tennis can be an emotional experience. Sometimes it's just impossible to stop the tears.

'I can cry like Roger. It's a shame I can't play like him,'

Andy Murray said after defeat to Federer in the 2010 Australian Open final.

ANDY MURRAY

Murray believes his tears after the 2012 Wimbledon final – a match he had lost to Federer – changed the public's perception of him. 'When I cried on Centre Court at Wimbledon after losing to Federer, some people saw me in a different light. People didn't laugh or think less of me. It was the opposite. It felt like they respected me more. They respected me for letting off the pressure cooker of emotion and for letting the mask slip.'

ROGER FEDERER

'Roger Blubberer' was one of the headlines in the British newspapers the morning after an emotional Federer won his first Grand Slam title at the 2003 Wimbledon Championships.

'God, this is killing me,'

Federer said as he wept during his speech after losing the 2009 Australian Open final to Rafael Nadal.

NOVAK DJOKOVIC

Paris can be a tough tennis crowd, so Djokovic was understandably moved when, after losing to Stan Wawrinka in the 2015 French Open final, he was given a two-minute ovation.

'It's not easy to handle,'

Djokovic said of losing in the first round of the 2016 Rio Olympics – he left the court in tears.

MARIN CILIC

Cilic's tears during the 2017 Wimbledon final were caused by a blister on his foot – he wasn't crying because of the physical pain, but because of the anguish of not being able to play his best against Federer.

RAFAEL NADAL

After his great rival, Federer, beat Robin Söderling in the 2009 French Open final to complete the career Grand Slam, Nadal became extremely emotional. 'Roger deserved to win all four Grand Slams and so I cried when he won Roland Garros. I was moved.'

IVAN LENDL

While Lendl didn't show much emotion during his playing career – hence the nickname of 'Old Stoneface' – he did cry after coaching Murray to the 2016 Wimbledon title. After first suggesting that the moisture in his eyes had been brought on by an allergy, he gave up and admitted they were tears of joy: 'Of course we are emotional, we are all busting our chops for Andy to do well and win. When it is achieved, it is a very good feeling.'

JANA NOVOTNÁ

The Czech sobbed on the Duchess of Kent's shoulder after losing the 1993 Wimbledon final to Steffi Graf.

STAN WAWRINKA

Tears can be expected after a Grand Slam final, but this Swiss player cried before stepping on court to play Novak Djokovic for the 2016 US Open title. 'Before the final, I was really nervous, like never before. I was shaking in the locker room. Five minutes before the match, I was talking to my coach and started to cry, and I was also completely shaking,' said Wawrinka, who went on to defeat Djokovic.

MARTINA HINGIS

When she lost the 1999 French Open final to Steffi Graf, Hingis burst into tears. After leaving the court, she had to be persuaded by her mother to return for the presentation ceremony.

RACKETS, STRINGS AND BALLS

From cows' intestines to 'spaghetti' rackets, to the
last player to win a Grand Slam with a wooden racket,
we take a look at the numbers.

3

The number of cows it takes to
string a tennis racket if you're
using natural gut, which is made
from cows' intestines.

40

The number of pairs – in millions
– of Adidas Stan Smiths that
have been sold. This makes it the
company's bestselling shoe of all
time (according to Adidas's annual
report). Stan Smith won his two
Grand Slam titles in the 1970s.

1967

The year that Billie Jean King,
with her stainless-steel frame
at the US Open, became the
first player to win a Grand Slam
singles title with a racket that
wasn't made of wood.

1983

The year that Yannick Noah
won the French Open title – he
was the last player to take a
Grand Slam singles title with
a wooden racket.

1986

The year that Wimbledon switched to yellow balls, having previously used the traditional white. That was 14 years after the International Tennis Federation (ITF) introduced yellow balls to the sport after research showed they were easier for the television viewer to follow on screen.

135–147

To comply with the ITF's standards, a tennis ball must bounce to a height of 135–147cm when dropped onto concrete from 254cm. The ball must also weigh 56–59.4g and have a diameter of 6.54–6.86cm. Balls fly faster in the heat and at altitude and are slower and heavier in humid conditions.

2

The ITF banned the double-strung or 'spaghetti' racket, an innovation from the 1970s that enabled a player to generate extreme amounts of spin.

300

The approximate number of tennis balls – in millions – that are manufactured globally each year.

ICON **STEFFI GRAF**

But for Serena Williams, Graf would be the most successful
female tennis player of the Open era. The German would run
around her backhand to smack the ball with her stronger
groundstroke, a strategy that led to her nickname.

THE FACTS

NICKNAME
Fräulein Forehand

DATE OF BIRTH
14 June 1969

BIRTHPLACE
Mannheim, former
West Germany

HEIGHT
1.76m (5ft 9½in)

PLAYING STYLE
Right-handed (one-
handed backhand)

1

The first and, to
date, only player,
man or woman, to
have accomplished
the Golden Slam
by winning all four
majors and the
Olympic gold medal
in the same
year. Graf's golden
year was 1988.

RECORDS

22

On her retirement, Graf's 22 Grand Slam singles titles put her ahead of any man or woman in the Open era. Serena Williams matched Graf's 22 in 2016, and then reached 23 by winning the 2017 Australian Open.

4

The first man or woman to win each Grand Slam four times or more.

377

Graf spent 377 weeks as the world number one, a record for both sexes.

186

She shares, with Serena Williams, the record for the longest time as number one – 186 consecutive weeks.

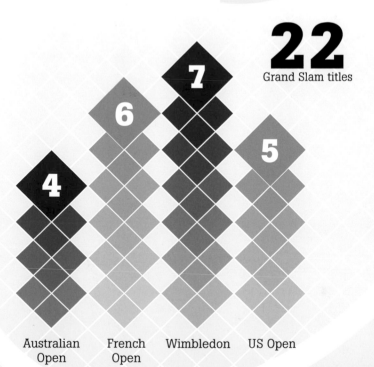

22
Grand Slam titles

7
6
5
4

Australian Open   French Open   Wimbledon   US Open

GRAF
IN NUMBERS

0

The number of people close to Graf who call her Steffi; she prefers 'Stefanie'.

3

Graf's age when she started playing tennis, using a wooden racket with a sawn-off handle, and under the instruction of her father, Peter. They sometimes hit balls over the sofa in their home – if the young Graf managed 25 in a row she was rewarded with strawberries and ice cream.

31

The number of times Graf was a finalist at one of the Grand Slams.

1

The number of occasions that a fan called out during a match at Wimbledon, 'Steffi, will you marry me?' and she responded: 'How much money do you have?'.

FASTEST FOREHANDS

Who has the fastest forehand? The numbers here are averages according to data published by Tennis Australia's Game Insight Group.

MEN

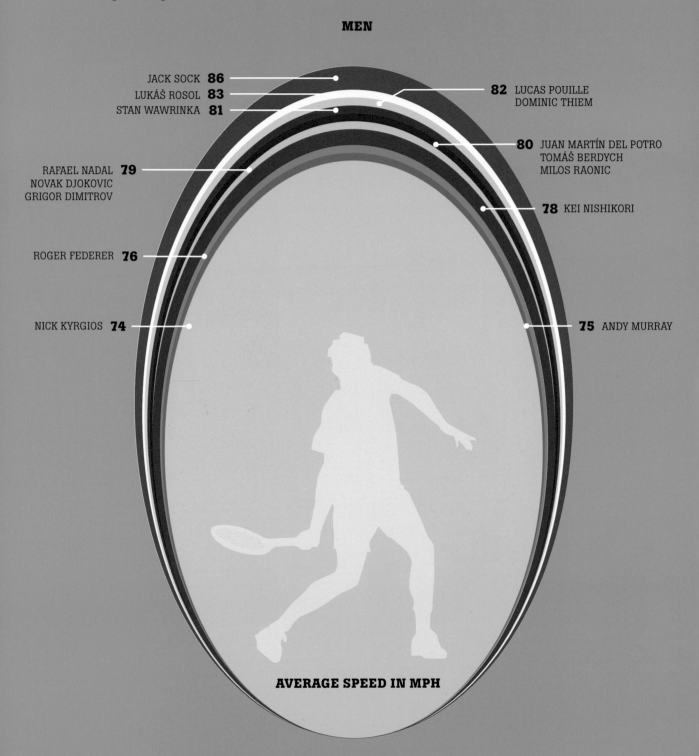

JACK SOCK **86**
LUKÁŠ ROSOL **83**
STAN WAWRINKA **81**

82 LUCAS POUILLE
DOMINIC THIEM

80 JUAN MARTÍN DEL POTRO
TOMÁŠ BERDYCH
MILOS RAONIC

RAFAEL NADAL **79**
NOVAK DJOKOVIC
GRIGOR DIMITROV

78 KEI NISHIKORI

ROGER FEDERER **76**

NICK KYRGIOS **74**

75 ANDY MURRAY

AVERAGE SPEED IN MPH

WOMEN

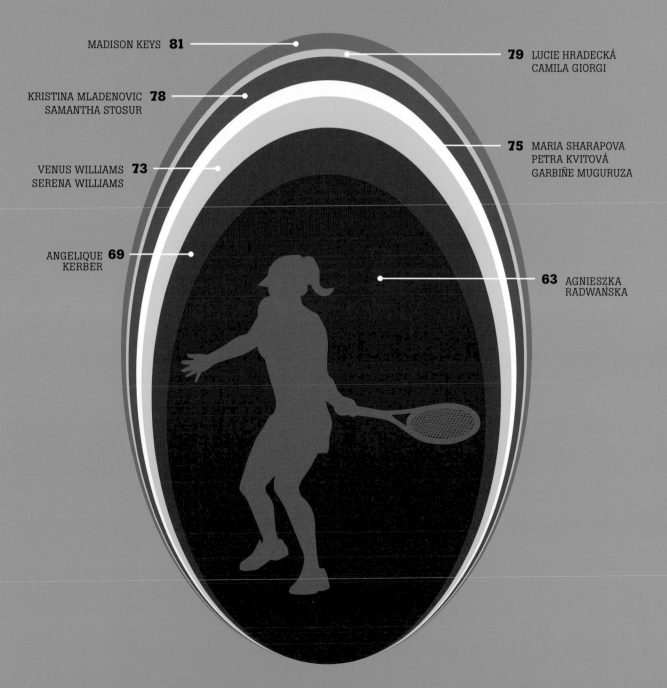

MADISON KEYS **81**

79 LUCIE HRADECKÁ
CAMILA GIORGI

KRISTINA MLADENOVIC **78**
SAMANTHA STOSUR

75 MARIA SHARAPOVA
PETRA KVITOVÁ
GARBIÑE MUGURUZA

VENUS WILLIAMS **73**
SERENA WILLIAMS

ANGELIQUE **69**
KERBER

63 AGNIESZKA
RADWAŃSKA

CHANGEOVER MOMENTS

Those 90 seconds should be an opportunity for rest and reflection before changing ends – but much can happen in a minute and a half.

Andy Murray and **Svetlana Kuznetsova** have both given themselves haircuts on court. Murray snipped off some of his fringe; Kuznetsova hacked at her ponytail.

Marcos Baghdatis was caught texting his wife during a changeover at the US Open. As use of mobile phones is prohibited during matches, he was warned for 'unsportsmanlike conduct'.

Fiction can invigorate tired minds – competing at the 1993 season finale in Frankfurt, **Jim Courier** spent the changeovers reading *Maybe the Moon*, a novel by Armistead Maupin. According to the *New York Times Book Review*, the book is about 'an overweight dwarf who longs to escape a stereotyped role in a famous film'. 'I read it out of desperation,' the American said. 'I was tired and looking for solutions. Most people were surprised it was real literature and not John Grisham.'

Karsten Braasch used to smoke cigarettes during the changeovers – it's said that the German's habit led to the ATP introducing a no-smoking rule on court.

Serena Williams once ordered a shot of espresso during a changeover – when the coffee arrived, she quickly drank it, and her game almost immediately picked up.

On a lively night at the 2005 Australian Open, **Juan Ignacio Chela** spat in **Lleyton Hewitt's** direction. According to Hewitt, Chela had become 'frustrated with me revving the crowd up and saying "C'mon".' The Argentine was later fined.

Much to **Andy Murray's** annoyance, television cameras have zoomed in on the changeover notes he has written for himself (including pointers such as 'stay calm and breathe'). His mother, Judy, called it 'disrespectful' and an 'invasion of privacy'.

Richard Gasquet spends many a changeover regripping his racket. The Frenchman, who doesn't think there is a faster regripper on tour, has been known to reapply the grip during each and every change of ends.

Suzanne Lenglen, the prima donna of the 1920s tennis scene, would sip brandy between games to calm her nerves.

Even after spending the changeovers reading a love letter from his wife, **Pete Sampras** couldn't avoid disaster at his final Wimbledon, in 2002. 'My husband, seven-times Wimbledon Champion, Pete, remember this,' the letter from his wife, the actress Bridgette Wilson, began, 'you truly are the greatest player ever to pick up a racket.' Sampras still lost that second-round match to George Bastl, a 'lucky loser' from Switzerland with a triple-digit ranking.

On-court coaching in the women's game isn't universally popular, and one of the most extraordinary exchanges came when an American player, **Alison Riske**, invited her boyfriend to advise her during a changeover. The microphones reportedly picked him up telling her to 'shut the ---- up'.

HOW TENNIS IS GETTING OLDER

Thirty used to be considered 'old' in tennis. 'Dirty thirty', they used to say. But that's all changed, with players now prospering until their mid-30s, and with the men's and women's tour older than ever before.

70

The combined age of the two singles champions at the 2017 Australian Open, with Roger Federer and Serena Williams both 35 years old. Federer was the oldest man to win a major since a 37-year-old Ken Rosewall scored the 1972 Australian Open, while Williams was the oldest female Grand Slam singles champion of the modern era. Federer retained the title in 2018 – when he was 36 years old.

31

In 2017, a 31-year-old Rafael Nadal became the oldest ever man to finish a season as the world number one.

43

In 2017, a record 43 players aged 30 or above finished in the ATP's top 100.

35

A 35-year-old Roger Federer won the 2017 Wimbledon title to become the oldest men's singles champion at the All England Club in the modern era.

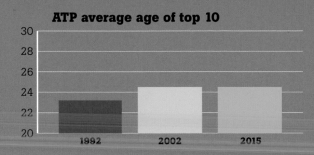

ATP average age of top 10

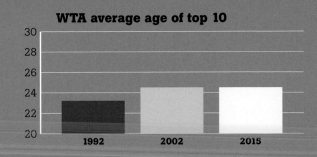

WTA average age of top 10

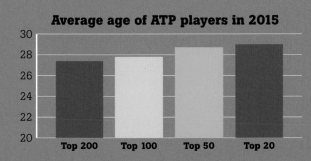

Average age of ATP players in 2015

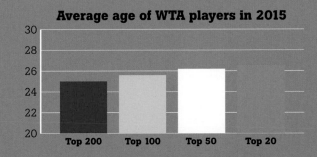

Average age of WTA players in 2015

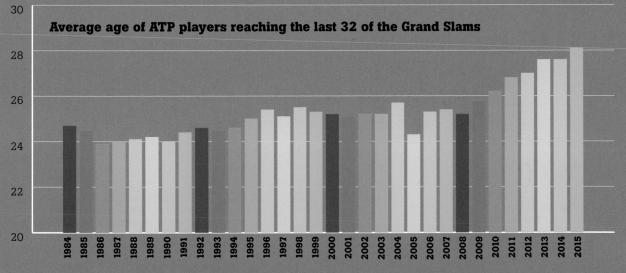

Average age of ATP players reaching the last 32 of the Grand Slams

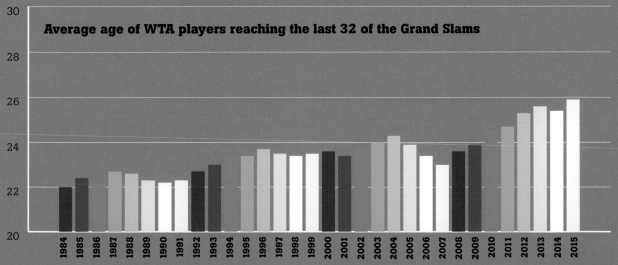

Average age of WTA players reaching the last 32 of the Grand Slams

TROPHIES

Ultimately, trophies are what everyone plays for – the chance to hold aloft the biggest prizes in tennis. Some of the trophies, though, are more unconventional than others, including a sword, a falcon and a silver pear.

The Venus Rosewater Dish, a silver salver that was first presented to the Wimbledon women's singles champion in 1886, is not an original design but a copy of a pewter dish kept in the Louvre in Paris. At the centre of the design is the mythological figure of Temperance, who is holding a lamp in one hand and a jug in the other.

The US Open men's and women's singles trophies are made by Tiffany & Co.

The champion in Acapulco in Mexico is given a large silver pear mounted on a black box.

A pineapple sits on top of the Wimbledon men's singles trophy, which was first presented in 1887; and no one knows why. One theory is that the fruit was a rarity at the time and so something of a status symbol. It may also owe something to the tradition of British naval captains putting a pineapple on their gateposts when returning from the seas. The inscription on the trophy reads: 'The All England Lawn Tennis Club Single Handed Champion of the World.'

At 105kg, the Davis Cup weighs more than most players. In Spain, the trophy is known as La Ensaladera, or The Salad Bowl.

The greatest diva in the history of the women's game, the 1920s icon Suzanne Lenglen, is commemorated with the trophy awarded to the women's singles champion at the French Open: La Coupe Suzanne Lenglen.

Both singles trophies at Roland Garros are named after players from the 1920s, with the men competing for La Coupe des Mousquetaires, or The Musketeers' Cup, which was redesigned in 1981. The Musketeers were a quartet of Frenchmen: Jacques Brugnon, Jean Borotra, Henri Cochet and René Lacoste.

The champion of the men's grass-court tournament in Stuttgart, Germany, receives a Mercedes, while the winner of the women's clay-court event in the same city gets to drive away in a Porsche.

Win the title in Doha, Qatar, and you'll receive a golden falcon trophy and a ceremonial sword.

A couple of days after winning his first Wimbledon title in 2003, Roger Federer appeared at a tournament in Switzerland, where he was presented with something unusual – a cow called Juliette.

There's a tragic story behind the Daphne Akhurst Memorial Cup, which is presented to the women's singles champion at the Australian Open. Akhurst won five titles at the Australian Open from 1925 to 1930 but died in 1933, at the age of just 29, after an ectopic pregnancy. The trophy was first presented the following year.

The men's singles trophy at the Australian Open, the Norman Brookes Challenge Cup, is named after a former champion. First presented in 1934, it's also a copy of an 8-tonne marble vase sculpted in the second century AD.

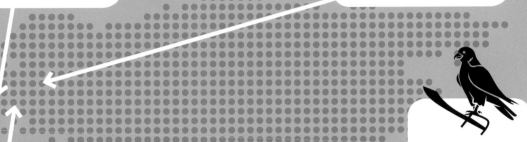

DOUBLES

Most professional tennis players like the one-on-one gladatorial nature of the sport. Others, though, prefer to have a teammate alongside them.

STANDARD FORMATION
The server stands on one side and their partner on the other, in the service box.

BOTH BACK
The server stands on one side and their partner on the other, at the baseline.

THE AUSTRALIAN FORMATION
Both the server and the partner start the point on the same side.

THE I-FORMATION
The server stands close to the centre of the court with their partner crouched on the centreline in the service box.

THE MOST SUCCESSFUL MEN'S DOUBLES TEAMS IN HISTORY

Bob and Mike Bryan
Grand Slam doubles titles as a team:

 **16**

Todd Woodbridge and Mark Woodforde
Grand Slam doubles titles as a team:

 **11**

THE MOST SUCCESSFUL WOMEN'S DOUBLES TEAMS IN HISTORY

Martina Navratilova and Pam Shriver
Grand Slam doubles titles as a team:

 **20**

Serena and Venus Williams
Grand Slam doubles titles as a team:

 **14**

Gigi Fernández and Natasha Zvereva
Grand Slam doubles titles as a team:

 **14**

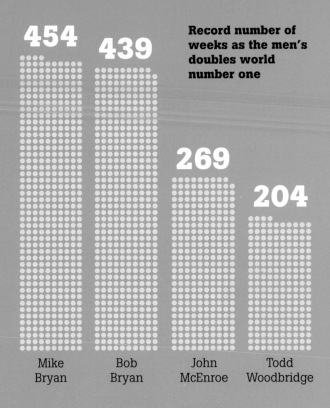

Record number of weeks as the men's doubles world number one

Mike Bryan	Bob Bryan	John McEnroe	Todd Woodbridge
454	439	269	204

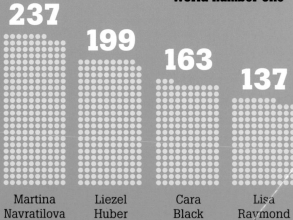

Record number of weeks as the women's doubles world number one

Martina Navratilova	Liezel Huber	Cara Black	Lisa Raymond
237	199	163	137

TENNIS AND POPULAR CULTURE

'They made me look like a jerk', John McEnroe complained after seeing the movie *Borg McEnroe*. But that's not the only occasion where there's been overlap between tennis and the arts.

1 John McEnroe so badly wanted to be a rock star – but his band didn't have critical or commercial success. 'At one gig,' McEnroe said, 'people threw tennis balls. At another, a guy in the audience yelled – and this was after our first song – "You suck". And then our equipment exploded.'

2 Andy Murray is the most unlikely of rappers, but there he is on the album produced by the tennis-playing twins, Bob and Mike Bryan. In a track entitled 'Autograph', Murray raps about the hardships of having to scribble his name: 'During Wimbledon, it gets really crazy, my mind cramps up and my mind gets hazy; sign and sign but the line doesn't end. Wake me up and let's do it again – autograph.'

3 Unlike Murray, Vince Spadea considered himself a dab hand at rapping. Displaying some of the bravado typical of this genre of music, the former top-20 player would rap: 'I'm Spadea and I ain't afraid of ya.' Inspired by one of his fellow Americans on the tour, Andy Roddick, Spadea produced these rhymes: 'Roddick is the hottest product, after I played him I needed an antibiotic. He's not robotic, but he's patriotic. I had a thought in my head, he hit a serve and I forgot it. Roddick, if he's in the tournament, you boycott it.'

4 The Williams sisters inspired Snoop Dogg, who rapped: 'You see Venus and Serena in the Wimbledon Arena.'

5 Serena Williams once appeared in the medical drama *ER* – she played a mother whose child was trapped inside a burning building.

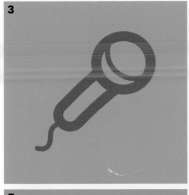

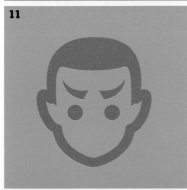

6 As House of Pain sang on their 1992 hit 'Jump Around': 'I'll serve your ass like John McEnroe.'

7 Yannick Noah may have won the 1983 French Open title, but for many he is now better known for his music, and once performed to 80,000 Parisians in the Stade de France. 'Don't ask me what's better, a big concert or winning trophies. It's like asking, "Do you like better the sunset or the sunrise?"'

8 Woody Allen's film *Match Point* tells the story of a retired tennis pro, played by Jonathan Rhys Meyers, who falls for Scarlett Johansson's character.

9 Alfred Hitchcock's *Strangers on a Train* is a film about a tennis player who makes a pact to commit murder with someone he meets during his rail journey.

10 'More raspberries than strawberries for this romantic comedy' is how one film critic assessed the 2004 movie *Wimbledon*, in which a British player (Paul Bettany) gets the girl (Kirsten Dunst) and wins the singles title.

11 Indian tennis player Vijay Amritraj played an MI6 agent in a James Bond film, *Octopussy*, as well as a starship officer in *Star Trek IV: The Voyage Home*.

12 Anna Kournikova made such an impression when she appeared in a music video for singer Enrique Iglesias that they soon started an off-screen relationship.

13 Serena Williams appeared in a music video for Beyoncé. 'They told me that they just wanted me to dance, like just really be free and just dance like nobody's looking and go all out.'

14 Rafael Nadal played the love interest in the video for Shakira's 2009 track, 'Gypsy'. As she sang to him: 'I'm a gypsy, are you coming with me? I might just steal your clothes and wear them if they fit me.'

ICON PETE SAMPRAS

Until Roger Federer ripped through the record books, Sampras was the most successful man in the history of tennis (and no one had a better slam-dunk smash). The American is truly one of the greats.

THE FACTS

NICKNAME
Pistol Pete

DATE OF BIRTH
12 August 1971

BIRTHPLACE
Washington DC,
United States

HEIGHT
1.85m (6ft 1in)

PLAYING STYLE
Right-handed (one-handed backhand)

12

The time, in years, between Sampras' first Grand Slam triumph, at the 1990 US Open, and his last, at the 2002 US Open, when he was 31 years old. So, Sampras was a Grand Slam champion in his teens, his twenties and his thirties.

RECORDS

6

The number of consecutive seasons Sampras finished top of the rankings – no other man has equalled that.

286

In all, he spent 286 weeks as the world number one, which was the record until Federer improved on that figure.

19

He is the youngest US Open men's singles champion in history – winning the 1990 title just days after turning 19.

7

Sampras was the first man in the modern era to win seven Wimbledon singles titles. Only Federer has won more.

14
Grand Slam titles

7

5

2

Australian Open   Wimbledon   US Open

SAMPRAS
IN NUMBERS

1

Sampras's racket stringer has said that if the leather grip shrank by just 1 millimetre, it would not escape Pete's notice (the tennis equivalent of *The Princess and the Pea*).

400

The approximate weight, in grams, of his customised racket, which is extremely heavy for a modern frame.

2

The number of years between his 13th major, at Wimbledon in 2000, and his 14th, in New York. During that time, Sampras considered retirement but was persuaded to continue by his wife, the actress Bridgette Wilson, who told him: 'Don't believe this crap that people are saying. Stop on your own terms. Just promise me that.'

9

The number of years that Sampras was out on his own with the record in men's tennis for the most major singles titles. He took that record at the 2000 Wimbledon Championships, moving beyond Roy Emerson's 12 titles, and he extended that tally to 14 at the 2002 US Open. In 2009, Sampras returned to Wimbledon, as a guest in the Royal Box, to watch Roger Federer beat Andy Roddick to score his 15th major.

TIMELINE OF GREATEST MALE PLAYERS

Here is a chart of the most successful male players of modern times, starting from when they each scored their first Grand Slam singles title. When Pete Sampras retired in 2002, he held the record for the most majors, with 14, but Roger Federer and Rafael Nadal have since eclipsed him, and Novak Djokovic could potentially become the third man to vault past the American.

YEAR

18 17 16 15 14 13 12 11 10 09 08 07 06 05 04 03 02 01 00 99 98 97 96 95 94 93 92 91 90

66

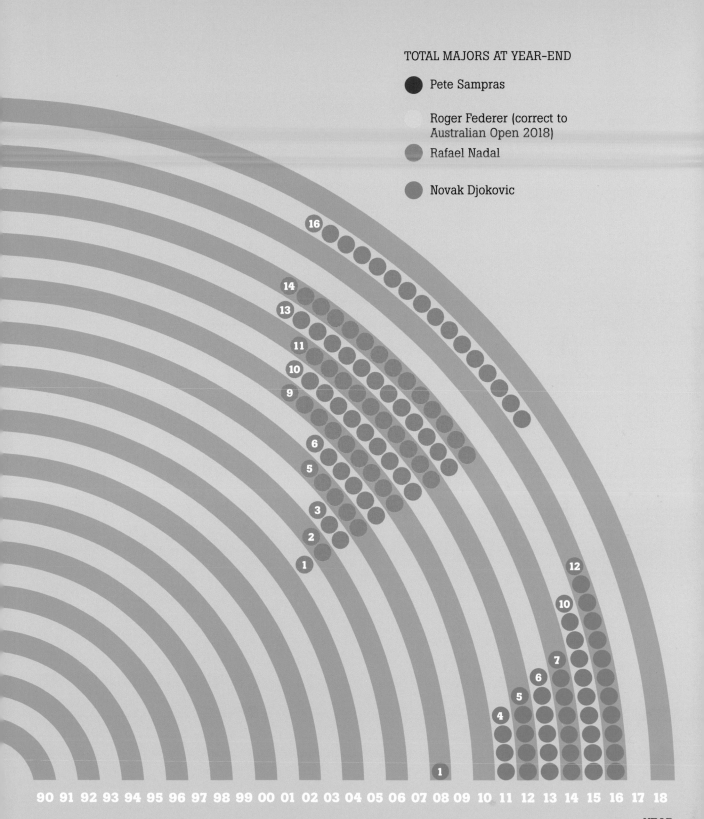

TOTAL MAJORS AT YEAR-END

● Pete Sampras

○ Roger Federer (correct to Australian Open 2018)

● Rafael Nadal

● Novak Djokovic

90 91 92 93 94 95 96 97 98 99 00 01 02 03 04 05 06 07 08 09 10 11 12 13 14 15 16 17 18

YEAR

THE MOST OUTLANDISH TENNIS FASHION

Tennis may be the most elegant of sports, but there have also been a few fashion mishaps and stylish surprises along the way.

SUZANNE LENGLEN
Roland Garros 1920s
Some tennis crowds were simply surprised, others were appalled – the Frenchwoman didn't just decline to wear a corset on court, she also flashed her ankles.

PAT STEWART
Wimbledon 1960s
With her telephone number embroidered on her knickers, the American caused quite a stir, with rumours that her boyfriend had 'dumped her' just before the tournament.

ANDRE AGASSI
Roland Garros 1990
'Hot lava' was Agassi's description of an outfit that included pink cycling shorts under black denim shorts. If that wasn't extraordinary enough, almost 20 years later Agassi disclosed that he had also been wearing a wig in his first Grand Slam final.

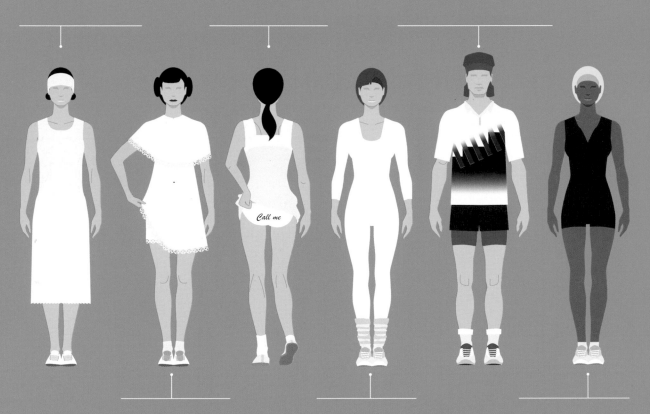

GERTRUDE MORAN
Wimbledon 1949
When 'Gorgeous Gussie' wore a short dress and lace-trimmed underwear, she was accused of 'putting sin and vulgarity into tennis'. The hysteria reached Westminster, with the knickers even discussed in Parliament.

ANNA WHITE
Wimbledon 1985
While it hadn't been her intention for 'anyone to spill their strawberries and cream', that was exactly what happened when the American player wore a controversial Lycra bodysuit.

SERENA WILLIAMS
US Open 2002
This black catsuit is probably Serena's most unusual outfit, even more daring than the T-shirt she wore after winning the 2009 Wimbledon title, emblazoned with the words 'Are you looking at my titles?'

DOMINIK HRBATY
US Open 2005
With two holes cut into
the back of his pink shirt,
revealing his shoulder
blades, the Slovakian
was certainly no slave to
convention. His fourth-
round conqueror, Lleyton
Hewitt, claimed 'No, I
wouldn't wear that shirt,
but it made it a lot easier
for me to beat him today.'

ROGER FEDERER
Wimbledon 2008
Eight years before
Federer was judged by *GQ*
magazine to be the world's
most stylish man of 2016,
he was known as the Lord
Cardigan of the Lawns.
Wearing a cardigan when
walking on to Centre Court,
he attracted comparisons
with Sebastian Flyte from
Brideshead Revisited.

STAN WAWRINKA
French Open 2015
Wawrinka's pink
tartan shorts became
such an integral part
of his run to the title
that he brought them
to his post-final news
conference and draped
them over the podium.

**BETHANIE
MATTEK-SANDS**
US Open 2007
Known as the Lady
Gaga of tennis, the
American has worn a
cowboy hat and NFL-
style antiglare patches
on court, although her
most courageous move
was a leopard-print
outfit.

VENUS WILLIAMS
Roland Garros 2010
A hint of Moulin Rouge
came to the clay when
Williams wore a red
and black lace outfit she
had designed herself (as
well as flesh-coloured
underwear).

**THE LITTLE
WHITE DRESS**
Wimbledon 2016
A Nike dress at
that summer's
championships caused
much controversy for
being too short, skimpy
and revealing. The
company later made
alterations.

THE FRENCH OPEN IN NUMBERS

Some would suggest that Roland Garros, also known as the French Open, is the most physically and emotionally demanding of the four Grand Slams. It's also the major with the hardest crowd to win over.

35

The number of games Rafael Nadal dropped all tournament in 2017, on the way to winning the title for a record tenth time.

116

MILLION

The Chinese audience for the 2011 women's singles final, when **Li Na** became the first Asian woman to win a Grand Slam singles title.

The number of champions who have been jeered by the toughest tennis crowd. He's the most successful clay-court player in history, but **Rafael Nadal** hasn't always been universally popular in Paris, and his uncle and coach, Toni, has spoken out against the crowd. **Serena Williams** has spoken of the extreme behaviour of the spectators, and **Maria Sharapova** was once so incensed that she said something very rude in a mixture of French and English. **Garbiñe Muguruza**, who won the 2016 title, was so upset with sections of the crowd during the 2017 tournament that she wept after the match.

0

The number of sliding roofs that can be closed in the event of wet weather. The French Open is the only Grand Slam without one to deploy over the centre court.

32

The time, in minutes, it took **Steffi Graf** to demolish **Natasha Zvereva** 6-0, 6-0 in the 1988 final – in her champion's speech, the German apologised to the crowd for the brevity of the match.

21

The size of the Roland Garros venue in acres, making it the smallest of all the Grand Slam venues.

The number of ball boys and girls.

250

600

The number of prisoners that were held in Roland Garros during the Second World War, when the site was used by the French government as an internment and transit camp.

31

The number of consecutive matches that **Rafael Nadal** had won at Roland Garros before he lost on the clay courts for the first time – against Sweden's **Robin Söderling** in the fourth round of the 2009 tournament.

Michael Chang's age when he became the youngest men's Grand Slam singles champion (a record he still holds). Chang's run to the title in 1989 is mostly remembered for the underarm serve he hit against Ivan Lendl in the fourth round.

25 MINUTES

The time that the groundstaff spend watering each court in the evening – to prevent the brick dust from blowing away, and to retain the colour. The courts are watered between sets, when the staff also sweep the court and brush the lines. The clay court was invented in the late 19th century by two English brothers, William and Ernest Renshaw, as their grass court in the south of France kept on being singed by the Cannes sun. To protect the turf, they covered it with crushed terracotta pots.

2

2mm

6–7cm

7–8cm

30cm

The depth, in millimetres, of the red brick dust that is dusted on top of the court surface. Scrape away that coating and you will find 6–7cm of crushed white limestone and, going deeper still, 7–8cm of clinker, or coal residue, at least 30cm of crushed gravel and a drain.

1.1

The amount of clay, in tonnes, needed for one court, although that figure is higher for the main stadium, Court Philippe Chatrier, which, with its larger run-offs behind the baselines, requires 1.5 tonnes.

ICONIC SHOTS

Boris Becker will forever be remembered for his diving volley, and Pete Sampras for his slam-dunk smash. Which other shots have achieved iconic status?

'Nasty' was Andre Agassi's assessment of **Rafael Nadal**'s topspin forehand.

Pete Sampras would employ his slam-dunk smash to scare his opponents. 'I used to play the shot for a whole bunch of reasons and one of them was intimidation. It's sending out a message to your opponent that says, "I'm moving well, I'm feeling good, and you're not going to get anything past me today".'

'A great liquid whip' was how the late American writer David Foster Wallace described **Roger Federer**'s forehand.

For all his grace and class on a tennis court, **Federer** can also be cheeky – hence his fondness for playing a 'tweener'.

Martina Navratilova's greatness was built around the brilliance of her volley – no one before or since has been in such command in the service box.

'It's like he is serving out of a tree,' Andy Roddick once observed of the 2.11m (6ft 11in) tall **Ivo Karlović.**

Boris Becker could never resist the opportunity to play a diving volley: 'I dived on all surfaces, and believe me, diving on hard courts is painful, but I just couldn't stop myself. It just became something I did, a part of my game.'

Stan Wawrinka's single-handed backhand has style and power – John McEnroe suggested it might just be the finest backhand the sport has ever seen.

'The greatest weapon in tennis history,' John McEnroe said of **Serena Williams'** serve.

Steffi Graf was forever running around her backhand to play inside-out forehands, which was why she became known as 'Fräulein Forehand'. 'My forehand was my strength,' she once observed.

ICON **NOVAK DJOKOVIC**

For so many years, Djokovic was the third man of the Federer–Nadal era – and then he transformed himself into one of the greats. At his peak, Djokovic was arguably more dominant than Federer or Nadal had ever been.

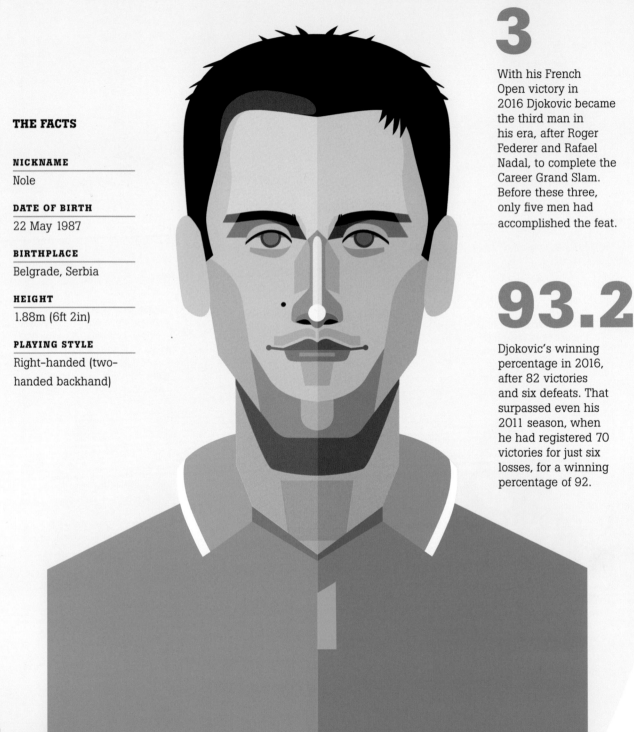

THE FACTS

NICKNAME
Nole

DATE OF BIRTH
22 May 1987

BIRTHPLACE
Belgrade, Serbia

HEIGHT
1.88m (6ft 2in)

PLAYING STYLE
Right-handed (two-handed backhand)

3

With his French Open victory in 2016 Djokovic became the third man in his era, after Roger Federer and Rafael Nadal, to complete the Career Grand Slam. Before these three, only five men had accomplished the feat.

93.2

Djokovic's winning percentage in 2016, after 82 victories and six defeats. That surpassed even his 2011 season, when he had registered 70 victories for just six losses, for a winning percentage of 92.

RECORDS

47

With his victory at the 2016 French Open, Djokovic became the first man for 47 years, since Rod Laver in 1969, to hold all four Grand Slams simultaneously.

3

He is the only man in the Open era to have won three successive Australian Open titles.

100 million

The first player in history to win US$100 million in prize money, a figure he reached at the 2016 French Open.

4

The only player to win four consecutive titles at the year-end ATP Finals.

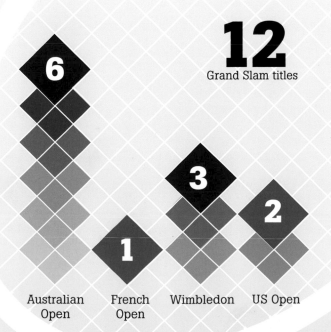

12

Grand Slam titles

6 Australian Open
1 French Open
3 Wimbledon
2 US Open

DJOKOVIC
IN NUMBERS

6

No man has won more Australian Open titles in the professional era than Djokovic, who has won six. Roger Federer matched this figure with victory at the 2018 tournament.

3

The number of times in a day that the air-raid siren would go off in Belgrade, as NATO bombed the city in 1999. Djokovic was 12 years old. 'We will never forget because it's just very deep inside of you . . .. We had the alarm noise about planes coming to bomb us every single day, so a minimum of three times a day, for two and a half months. There was huge noise in the city all the time, all the time. ... when I hear a big noise even now, I get a little traumatised.'

17

The number of consecutive finals Djokovic reached, in the 12 months from the 2015 Australian Open to the 2016 Australian Open.

43

The number of consecutive matches that he won across the 2010–11 season, which was only just three wins short of Guillermo Vilas's record 46-match run, back in 1977.

BIZARRE AND UNEXPECTED INJURIES

Roger Federer sustained the worst injury of his career while he was running a bath for his children. And he wasn't the first or the last tennis player to suffer a bizarre or unexpected injury.

Eugenie Bouchard sued the United States Tennis Association after falling over in the physiotherapy room at the US Open, claiming that there had been a 'slippery, foreign and dangerous' substance on the floor.

American Lauren Davis was stung on the bottom by a wasp while playing a tournament in Miami.

Keeping cool on court is important, but for Kristýna Plíšková, who was competing in China at the time, it resulted in injury, with the Czech damaging her thumb after getting too close to a large fan behind the umpire's chair.

Days after winning the 2010 Wimbledon title, Serena Williams was in a restaurant in Munich when she cut her foot on some glass from a broken beer bottle. 'I saw a specialist in New York and he said that I didn't have to fix it, but that I would have a droopy toe for the rest of my life. So I decided to have the surgical procedure, for my career and for my life.'

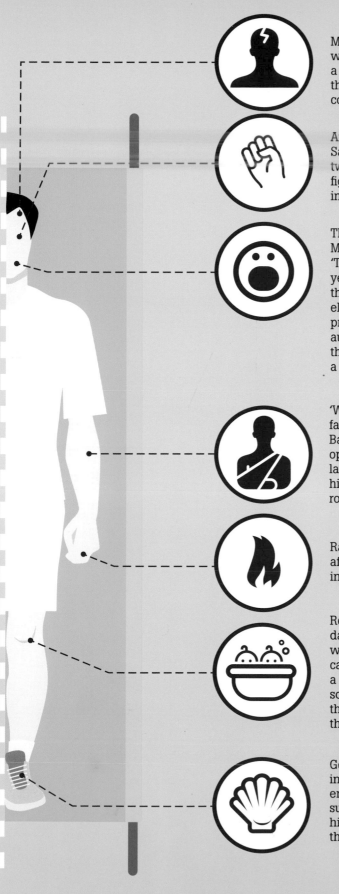

Mikhail Youzhny bashed himself about the head with his racket after missing a break point during a match in Miami. With his face covered in blood, the Russian needed a medical timeout before he could continue.

An off-season brawl in Moscow meant that Marat Safin arrived at his first tournament of 2009 with two black eyes and cuts to his face. 'I won the fight, I'm good, I'm OK,' he said. 'I got in trouble in Moscow but it's OK, I can survive.'

The prospect of playing Wimbledon leaves Andy Murray with a mouth full of ulcers every summer. 'They come on before the Championships every year, the sign that, although I try to block out all that the tournament means to me and to everyone else in the country, my body will respond to the pressure in a way I can't control,' he wrote in his autobiography. 'The ulcers tend to disappear by the time the event comes around, but they are a painful reminder of the time of year.'

'Worst day of my life,' Sam Querrey tweeted after falling through a glass table at a tournament in Bangkok. The American, who needed an arm operation, made a full recovery and several years later supplied one of the greatest shocks in tennis history by beating Novak Djokovic in the third round of the 2016 Wimbledon Championships.

Rafael Nadal played with bandages on his fingers after burning his hand at a Japanese restaurant in the United States.

Roger Federer was running a bath for his twin daughters when he heard a click in his knee – he would end up having the first operation of his career and missing half of the 2016 season. 'It was a movement that you do, I do, 20 times a day and so it could have happened when I was crossing the road. I just turned my knee a little bit and that was that.'

Goran Ivanišević was strolling along a beach in Miami when a piece of seashell became embedded in his foot, which then required surgery. There was also the time he was leaving his apartment and his hand became trapped in the door – a finger broke in three places.

TENNIS FAMILIES

The Williams sisters, the Murray brothers, the Bryan twins, the McEnroe brothers – let's take a look at some of the most accomplished tennis families.

1 It was fitting that, when Serena became the most successful female player of modern times – with her victory at the 2017 Australian Open taking her to 23 Grand Slams, a record for the Open era – her opponent that day was her big sister. As Serena said of Venus: 'She's my inspiration. She's the only reason the Williams sisters exist.'

2 The Murrays were the first brothers in tennis history to both hold world number one rankings – Jamie in doubles and Andy in singles. 'I think Andy has a lot to thank Jamie for,' their mother Judy has said. 'Jamie was just a little bit older, and a bit better, and Andy was always striving to keep up.'

3 With their 'twin energy', Bob and Mike Bryan – who are identical apart from one being a right-hander and the other a lefty – became the most successful doubles team in men's tennis history.

4 'When you're not doing well and people wanted to talk to you about your brother, you just want to go hide under a rock.' So said Patrick McEnroe, John's brother. John was a number one for singles and doubles, while Patrick peaked at number three in doubles.

5 Between them, the Renshaw brothers won eight Wimbledon singles titles, all in the 19th century. William snaffled seven and Ernest one.

6 Zimbabwean Cara Black was a doubles number one, as was her brother Byron. Their brother Wayne reached number four in the standings. Amazingly, all three siblings won Grand Slam doubles titles.

7 In 2017, Alexander and Mischa Zverev became the first brothers since 1991 to both finish a season in the singles top 35.

8 Marat Safin and Dinara Safina were the first brother and sister to both achieve the world number one singles ranking. Safina once said of her brother, 'When you play, I love watching you. When you lose, I'm even sadder than when I lose. When you're hurt, I suffer. When you talk to me, I drink your words. When you come to see me play, I'm beside myself with joy.'

9 Arantxa Sánchez Vicario was a number one for singles and doubles, and her brother Emilio also held the top ranking for doubles, while another sibling, Javier, achieved a top-10 doubles ranking.

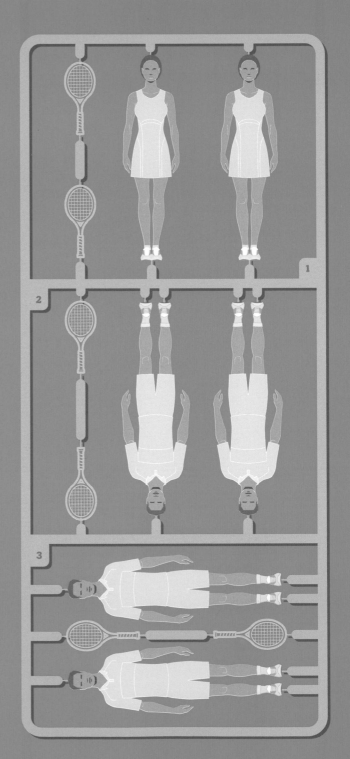

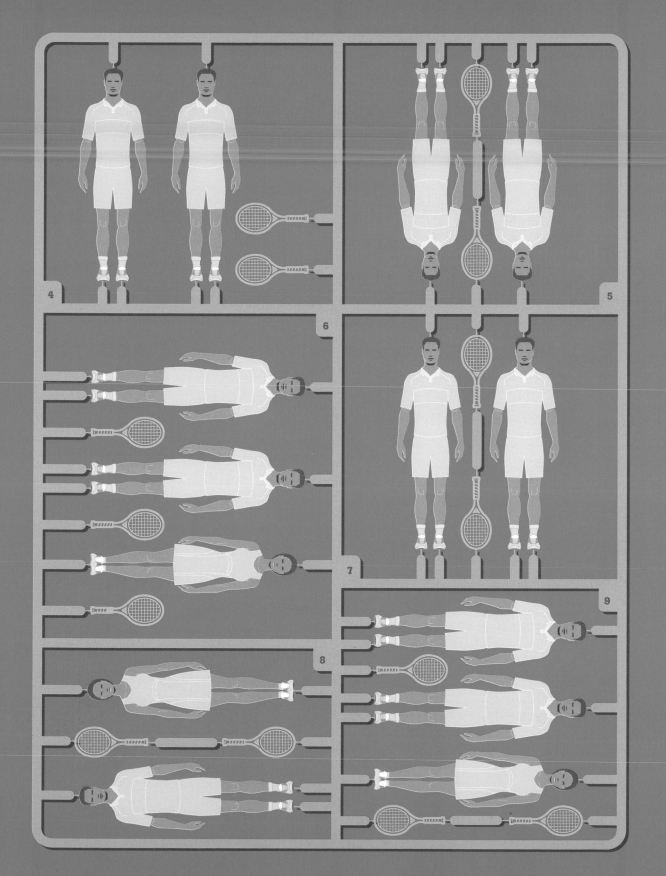

TIE-BREAK SPECIAL

Nothing reveals a player's mental strengths – or weaknesses – in the way that a tie-break does. Just one blooper on your own serve and the set could be lost. But just one moment of inspiration or brilliance to achieve a mini-break, and the set, and perhaps the match, could be yours. Which players have shown the greatest mental fortitude over the years?

SUDDEN DEATH

Tennis history was changed forever when a wealthy, eccentric American Jimmy Van Alen – who would become known as the 'Rolls-Royce rebel' – missed cocktail hour at his country club due to matches running too long. Jimmy's solution was to create a 'Sudden Death' tie-break, with the winner being the first player to reach five points. What could be more dramatic than a scoreline that reached 4-4 in Sudden Death, with everything on the line?

US OPEN

Sudden Death was first brought to the Grand Slams at the 1970 US Open. Just to add to the theatre, red flags and banners would be unfurled as the action took place.

LINGERING DEATH

For some players, this was almost too exciting – their nerves couldn't cope – and the tie-break was subsequently changed to its current format, with the winner being the first to seven points, provided he or she is two points ahead. Van Alen preferred the original, calling the new version 'Lingering Death'.

THE LONGEST TIE-BREAK (UNOFFICIALLY)

Two men from Monaco played a 70-point tie-break at the lowest level of men's professional tennis, in the qualifying round of a third-tier Futures tournament. Unfortunately, Benjamin Balleret's 36–34 tie-break against Guillaume Couillard, played in Florida in 2013, has no official status, as the match wasn't played with an umpire or line judges.

MEN'S RECORD

At a Futures tournament in Kazakhstan in 2016, Russia's Evgeny Tyurnev beat Serbia's Danilo Petrović after a 48-point tie-break in the first set.

WOMEN'S RECORD

Finland's Jenny Saarnilina was beaten by Clara Schuhmacher-Terron from Spain after a 27-25 tie-break in a 2005 singles qualifying match at an ITF Pro Circuit $10,000 tournament in Mollerussa, Spain.

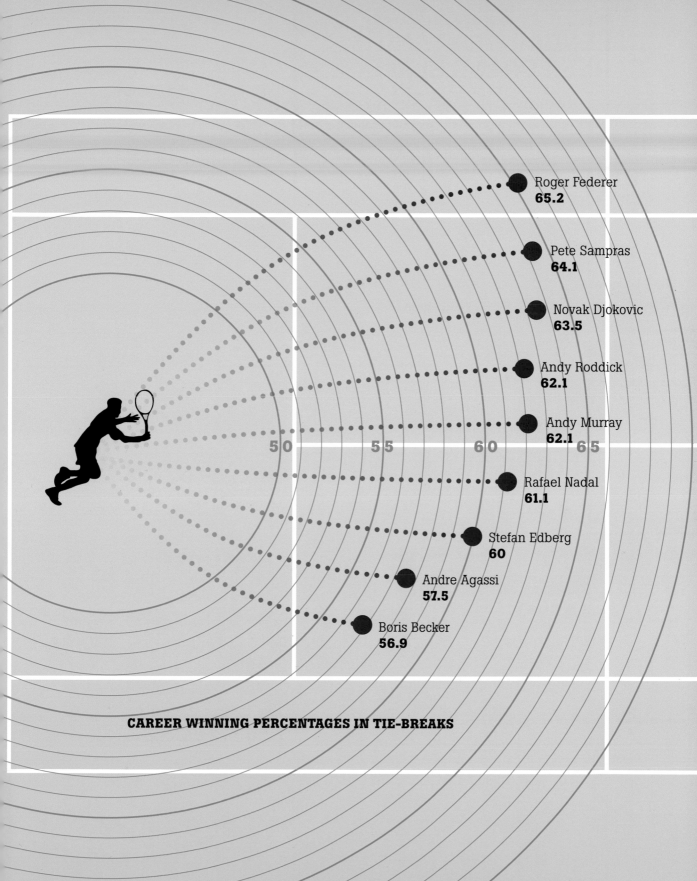

Roger Federer
65.2

Pete Sampras
64.1

Novak Djokovic
63.5

Andy Roddick
62.1

Andy Murray
62.1

Rafael Nadal
61.1

Stefan Edberg
60

Andre Agassi
57.5

Boris Becker
56.9

50   55   60   65

CAREER WINNING PERCENTAGES IN TIE-BREAKS

81

CALENDAR-YEAR AND CAREER GRAND SLAM

There's an exclusive group of players who have won all four Grand Slam titles. Even more exclusive than that is the small club of players who have scored all four in the same calendar year. And then there is a certain German female player who has done all that – and more.

CAREER GOLDEN SLAM
Winning all four majors and the Olympic title.

Men:
Andre Agassi ▲
Rafael Nadal

Women:
Steffi Graf
Serena Williams

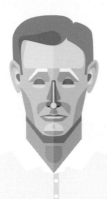

CALENDAR-YEAR GRAND SLAM
Only five players have won all four majors in the same season, with Rod Laver the sole player to do so twice.

Men:
Don Budge 1938
Rod Laver 1962/1969 ▲

Women:
Maureen Connolly 1953
Margaret Court 1970
Steffi Graf 1988

Steffi Graf
She is the only player, man or woman, to have accomplished the calendar-year Golden Slam.

CAREER GRAND SLAM

Eight men and 10 women have accomplished the Career Grand Slam.

Don Budge 22*
Rod Laver 24
Rafael Nadal 24
Fred Perry 26
◀ **Roger Federer** 27
Roy Emerson 27
Novak Djokovic 29
Andre Agassi 29

Maureen Connolly 18
• **Steffi Graf** 19
Margaret Court 20
Serena Williams 21
Maria Sharapova 25
Martina Navratilova 26
Chris Evert 27
Billie Jean King 28 ▶
Doris Hart 28
Shirley Fry Irvin 29

*age Career Grand Slam achieved

CAREER BOX SET

Winning the singles, doubles and mixed doubles titles at all four majors (no man has ever done this):

Margaret Court
Doris Hart
Martina Navratilova ▶

YOU CANNOT BE SERIOUS!

John McEnroe isn't the only tennis player who has misbehaved – and been punished for it. Here are some of the biggest fines in the history of tennis.

9 $20,000 – **Boris Becker** was punished in 1995 for appearing to suggest that Thomas Muster had taken performance-enhancing drugs.

8 $27,500 – **Fabio Fognini** received the largest fine in Wimbledon's history for three offences in one match at the 2014 Championships: making an obscene gesture, using abusive language and, worst of all, hitting the court with his racket (most of the fine was for damaging the lawn).

JOHN McENROE
$17,500

10 The largest fine of McEnroe's career came at the 1987 US Open on account of the obscene and abusive language he used during his third-round match against Slobodan Živojinović. As well as spewing abuse at the umpire and the linesmen, the New Yorker also turned on a television soundman. As the player himself admitted, he had been just 'one bad word from a default', but, soon after winning the match, he discovered he had been heavily fined and had also earned himself a two-month suspension from the tour.

7 $35,000 – In a ungentlemanly incident in Montreal in 2015, **Nick Kyrgios** sledged Stan Wawrinka, insinuating that the Swiss' girlfriend had been on intimate terms with Thanasi Kokkinakis. Kyrgios was fined $10,000 then an additional $25,000, withheld providing he met certain conditions over the next 6 months, which he did.

6 $56,000 – When **David Nalbandian** kicked an advertising board during the 2012 Queen's Club final, he couldn't have foreseen what would happen next. The board broke into several pieces, one of which pierced the leg of a line judge, who started to bleed heavily. Nalbandian was defaulted from the match, fined and docked his prize money (included in the headline figure).

JOHN McENROE $17,500 **10**

BORIS BECKER $20,000 **9**

FABIO FOGNINI $27,500 **8**

NICK KYRGIOS $35,000 **7**

DAVID NALBANDIAN $56,000 **6**

5 $63,000 - During a third-round match at the 1995 Wimbledon Championships, **Jeff Tarango** became so infuriated with the umpire Bruno Rebeuh that he accused him of being 'the most corrupt official in the game'. And that wasn't all; the American told the crowd to 'shut up' and walked off the court without finishing the match against Germany's Alexander Mronz. Tarango's wife also later admitted to having slapped the umpire across the face.

4 $100,000 - In 2011 **Dani Koellerer** was given a life ban, and a six-figure fine, for match-fixing offences. A controversial figure, known as 'Crazy Dani', and so unpopular with his peers that some of them once tried to have him thrown off the circuit, the Austrian appealed to the Court of Arbitration for Sport - while the ban stood, he didn't have to pay the fine.

3 $106,000 - **Lleyton Hewitt** was fined for allegedly not turning up for a television interview during the 2002 Cincinnati Masters, although the fine reduced to $20,000 on appeal.

2 $120,000 - **Fabio Fognini**, an Italian who describes himself as a 'hothead', was initially fined $24,000 for a derogatory remark towards a female umpire at the 2017 US Open. A few weeks later, the Italian was fined a further $96,000, though there was the possibility of that punishment being reduced if he behaved himself (he was also given a suspended ban from two Grand Slams).

SERENA WILLIAMS
$175,000

1 In John McEnroe's analysis, 'all hell broke loose' on the night Serena Williams lost to Kim Clijsters in the semi-finals of the 2009 US Open, with the American threatening a line judge who had called her for a foot fault: 'I swear to god, I'll ------- take the ball and shove it down your ------- throat.' In the end, she only paid $82,500 as the rest was suspended.

JEFF TARANGO $63,000

DANI KOELLERER $100,000

LLEYTON HEWITT $106,000

FABIO FOGNINI $120,000

SERENA WILLIAMS $175,000

5 **4** **3** **2** **1**

ICON MARTINA NAVRATILOVA

On and off the court, Navratilova transformed tennis. During the Cold War, she defected from communist Czechoslovakia, choosing to move to the West and become an American citizen. In all, Navratilova gathered 59 Grand Slam titles, the last of which she won when she was almost 50 years old.

THE FACTS

NICKNAME
The Great Wide Hope

DATE OF BIRTH
18 October 1956

BIRTHPLACE
Prague, former
Czechoslovakia

HEIGHT
1.73m (5ft 8in)

PLAYING STYLE
Left-handed (one-handed backhand)

167

Navratilova holds the record of singles titles for both sexes.

9

She has won more Wimbledon singles titles – nine in all – than any other player, man or woman. Six of those were won over consecutive years, also a record.

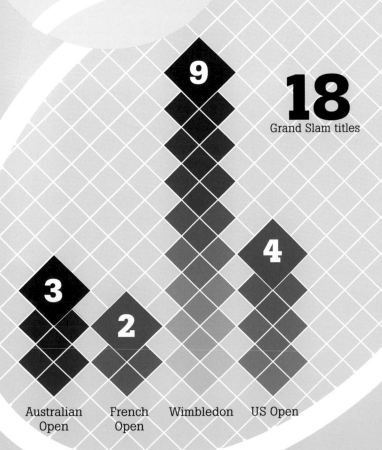

RECORDS

177

No man or woman has won more doubles titles than Navratilova, who gathered 177.

50

The oldest winner of a Grand Slam trophy – she was almost 50 years old when she won the mixed doubles title at the 2006 US Open with Bob Bryan.

237

Navratilova spent an unequalled 237 weeks as the doubles world number one. She also holds the record for the longest run at the top of the doubles rankings – 191 consecutive weeks.

9

18
Grand Slam titles

4

3

2

Australian Open

French Open

Wimbledon

US Open

NAVRATILOVA
IN NUMBERS

18

Navratilova's age when she defected from the former Czechoslovakia to the United States, while she was in New York to play in the 1975 US Open.

59

Navratilova's total number of Grand Slam trophies, with 18 singles triumphs, 31 women's doubles and 10 mixed doubles (second only to Margaret Court's 62 majors). She has a career box set from the Grand Slams – winning the singles, women's doubles and mixed doubles titles at all four majors.

332

The number of weeks she spent as the singles world number one.

58

Navratilova's age when she got married for the first time, to Julia Lemigova.

74

Navratilova won 74 consecutive matches in 1984, the longest winning streak in the Open era (in men's and women's tennis).

NICKNAMES

You're nobody in tennis if you don't have a nickname. Here's a selection of the somebodies.

THE WILD THING
An apt name given to the unpredictable Nick Kyrgios by the Australian media.

PSYCHO SERENA
The nickname that Serena Williams has given to one of her multiple personalities. 'Psycho Serena' plays the matches, apparently.

THE SCUD
Mark Philippoussis earned this nickname on account of the great power – and occasional waywardness – of his missile-like serve.

THE GREAT WIDE HOPE
The name given to a teenage Martina Navratilova by an American journalist after she defected to the United States and discovered fast food.

RUSTY
Lleyton Hewitt was given this nickname by his then coach, Darren Cahill, as Hewitt reminded him of Rusty Griswold from the *National Lampoon* movies of the 1980s.

DELICIANO

Feliciano López was given this nickname by Andy Murray's mother, Judy, with Murray himself commenting: 'I think it's about time she stopped that nonsense. It's making me throw up – it's disgusting.'

THE NINJA

Agnieszka Radwanska is known for slicing up opponents like a Japanese warrior.

THE MERCHANT OF MENACE

That, and McBrat, McNasty, Superbrat and the Incredible Sulk, were all names given to John McEnroe by the media.

BAMM-BAMM

As a child, Andy Murray was named after the destructive, adopted son of Barney and Betty Rubble from *The Flintstones*. 'I used to get so angry, I'd just be bashing things about.'

THE SPICE GIRLS OF TENNIS

Doubles partners Martina Hingis (above) and Anna Kournikova came up with their own playful nickname.

TOMIC THE TANK ENGINE

This was the name given to Bernard Tomic after he was accused of not giving his all on court.

GOOD GORAN

One of the voices in Goran Ivanišević's head when he won the 2001 Wimbledon title. 'Good Goran' was forever bickering with 'Bad Goran', so sometimes 'Emergency Goran' had to step in.

THE ZEN MASTER

This was Barbra Streisand's nickname for Andre Agassi.

THE DECLINE OF SERVE AND VOLLEY

Serve-and-volleying is out of fashion. But players should think again – you only have to look at the numbers to see it's a smart strategy.

5% 2002

5% 2003

4% 2004

4% 2005

4% 2006

2% 2007

2% 2008

2% 2009

2% 2010

2% 2011

1% 2012
2013
2014
2015
2016

WOMEN'S SINGLES MATCHES AT WIMBLEDON the percentage of serve-and-volley points

Men's singles
serve-and-volley success rate

68.2%

Women's singles
serve-and-volley success rate

65.9%

Wimbledon
When players serve-and-volley at Wimbledon, it's a successful tactic. In men's singles matches 68.2 per cent of serve-and-volley points were won by the server from 2002 to 2016. For comparison, men won 45.7 per cent of points from the baseline.

In women's singles matches 65.9 per cent of serve-and-volley points were won by the server from 2002 to 2016. For comparison, women won 47 per cent of points from the baseline.

2002 33%

2003 25%

2004 22%

Men's singles
serve-and-volley success rate

66.5%

US Open
Men serve-and-volleyed on 4 per cent of points played at the 2015 and 2016 US Opens, winning 66.5 per cent of those points. For comparison, players who stayed on the baseline won 46.5 per cent of points.

MEN'S SINGLES MATCHES AT WIMBLEDON
the percentage of serve-and-volley points

2005 19%

Men's singles
serve-and-volley success rate

65.5%

2006 14%

2007 12%

2008 10%

2009 10%

2010 8%

2011 6%

2012 6%

Australian Open
Men serve-and-volleyed on six per cent of points played at the 2016 and 2017 Australian Opens, winning 65.5 per cent of those points. For comparison, players who stayed on the baseline won 46.5 per cent of points.

Women's singles
serve-and-volley success rate

67.5%

2013 8%

2014 8%

Women serve-and-volleyed on 0.5 per cent of points played at the 2016 and 2017 Australian Opens, winning 67.5 per cent of those points. For comparison, players who stayed on the baseline won 48 per cent of points.

2015 10%

2016 10%

DAVIS CUP AND FED CUP ... IN NUMBERS

Tennis is an individual sport. Unless, that is, you are representing your country. Then, the pinnacle is team victory in the Davis Cup, for men, and the Fed Cup, for women.

1937

A few minutes before going on court to play Don Budge of the United States in a Davis Cup tie in 1937, Germany's Baron Gottfried von Cramm received a phone call from Adolf Hitler. Much to Hitler's displeasure, von Cramm lost that match, which was played at Wimbledon with the Swastika flying over Centre Court. The next year, the bisexual Prussian aristocrat was imprisoned for 'sex irregularities'.

27,488

The number of spectators who attended one day of the 2014 Davis Cup final in Lille, which saw Roger Federer's Switzerland defeat France. That is a record for the competition.

2007

The year that Germany's Tommy Haas believed he had been poisoned when playing a Davis Cup semi-final against Russia in Moscow. Exploring the possibility that there had been poison in his dessert or macchiato, Haas underwent toxicology tests but they came back negative.

2006

'Game, Sex and Match,' read the headline in *The Sun* newspaper after it emerged that Great Britain's team room at a Davis Cup tie in Odessa in Ukraine was part of a complex that had been used as a brothel. The room next door had pink decor, a bed and a mirrored ceiling.

DAVIS CUP

1974

The year that the Davis Cup final wasn't played, after India boycotted the tie with South Africa in protest against apartheid.

8

John McEnroe is the only player, since the introduction of the Davis Cup World Group in 1981, to have won a maximum eight singles rubbers in one year. He did so in 1982.

32

The number of times that the United States has won the Davis Cup, which is a record.

7,000

The estimated number of protesters when Sweden hosted Chile in Båstad in 1975. They were protesting against Augusto Pinochet's military regime.

1900

The year that the Davis Cup was first played, with the United States defeating a British team at Longwood Cricket Club in Boston, Massachusetts.

2017

The year that the United States Tennis Federation made the unfortunate error of playing a Nazi-era version of the German national anthem, the one including the line: '*Deutschland, Deutschland, über alles, über alles in der Welt.*' 'Horrifying and shocking, and the worst experience of my life,' said Germany's Andrea Petkovic. 'This is the year 2017 – that something like this happens in America, it can't happen. It's embarrassing and speaks of ignorance.'

37

The number of consecutive Fed Cup ties that the United States won from 1976 to 1983, which is a record.

29

Chris Evert won 29 consecutive singles rubbers for the United States from 1977 to 1986.

FED CUP

64

The number of consecutive Fed Cup rubbers that the United States won from 1978 to 1983, which is a record.

50

Spain's Arantxa Sánchez Vicario holds the record for the most Fed Cup singles victories.

18

The United States team is the most successful in the history of the Fed Cup, with 18 titles.

18

Arantxa Sánchez Vicario and Conchita Martinez won a record number of doubles rubbers as a pair.

1963

The year that the Fed Cup was first played, with the United States defeating Australia at Queen's Club in London.

HOW TENNIS IS GETTING TALLER

Has tennis become a sport for giants? That would probably be going too far, but there's no doubt that players are getting taller.

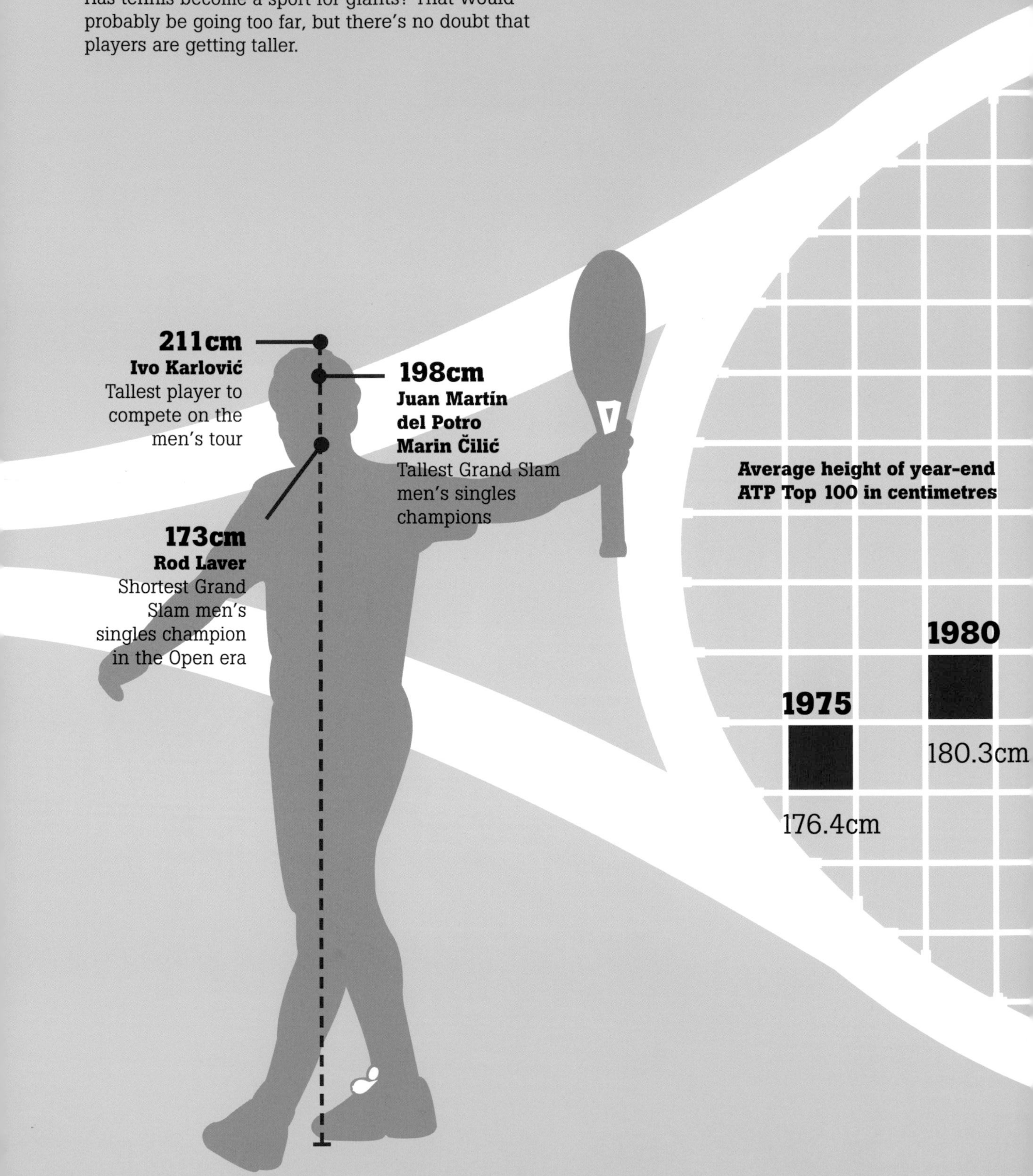

211cm
Ivo Karlović
Tallest player to compete on the men's tour

198cm
Juan Martín del Potro
Marin Čilić
Tallest Grand Slam men's singles champions

173cm
Rod Laver
Shortest Grand Slam men's singles champion in the Open era

Average height of year-end ATP Top 100 in centimetres

1980
180.3cm

1975
176.4cm

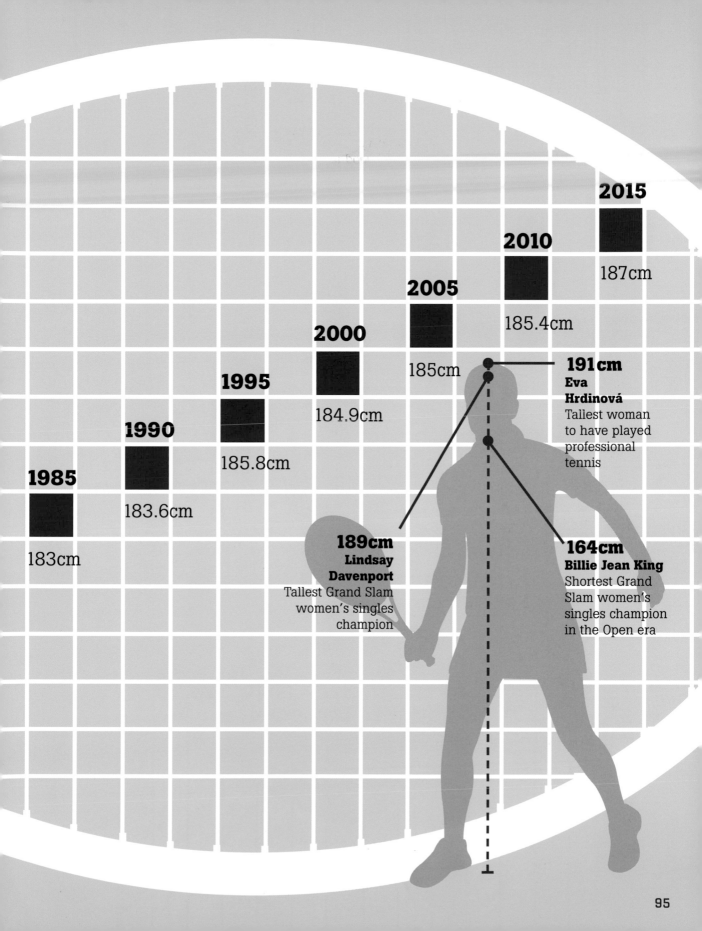

1985
183cm

1990
183.6cm

1995
185.8cm

2000
184.9cm

2005
185cm

2010
185.4cm

2015
187cm

191cm
Eva Hrdinová
Tallest woman to have played professional tennis

189cm
Lindsay Davenport
Tallest Grand Slam women's singles champion

164cm
Billie Jean King
Shortest Grand Slam women's singles champion in the Open era

ICON BJÖRN BORG

Has there been a calmer, more collected tennis player on court than the Swede? That cool persona and good looks helped him to become the first rock star of tennis.

THE FACTS

NICKNAME
The Ice Borg

DATE OF BIRTH
6 June 1956

BIRTHPLACE
Stockholm, Sweden

HEIGHT
1.80m (5ft 11in)

PLAYING STYLE
Right-handed (two-handed backhand)

35

Borg's resting heart rate, in beats per minute, according to the mythology that built up around the Swede. The reality, according to those close to him, was that his resting heart rate was around 50 beats per minute in the morning, and around 60 in the afternoon.

RECORDS

5

The first man in the modern era to win five successive Wimbledon titles.

6

Until Rafael Nadal's dominance at Roland Garros, no man in the modern era had won more French Open singles titles than Borg, who gathered six.

3

The number of years in succession, from 1978 to 1980, that Borg achieved the rare French Open–Wimbledon double in the same season.

28

The number of years that passed until someone else won the Paris and London majors in the same year; Nadal did so in 2008.

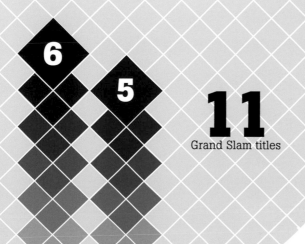

6

5

11
Grand Slam titles

French Open   Wimbledon

BORG
IN NUMBERS

26

The age at which Borg took premature retirement in 1983 (he would make a disastrous comeback in the early 1990s).

0

The number of sets Borg lost in his first Wimbledon final (against Ilie Nastase in 1976).

4

The number of times that Borg finished as runner-up at the US Open. The last of those defeats came in 1981. After losing to John McEnroe, Borg didn't even hang around for the prize-giving ceremony and instead immediately left for the airport, not even bothering to change out of his tennis clothes.

1

The number of times Borg played the Australian Open – his sole appearance came in 1974, when he made the third round.

5

The number of Borg's Wimbledon trophies – so all of them – that he put up for sale in 2006 with an auction house in London (along with a couple of rackets). When McEnroe found out, he immediately called Borg and questioned the decision. Borg reconsidered and promised he would never sell the trophies.

IT'S A SCANDAL!

Like all big sports, tennis has had more than a few scandalous moments.
Here are some of the most controversial episodes in its history.

BORED

The Wimbledon grass is supposed to inspire players to ever greater heights, but the lawns didn't do much for Bernard Tomic at the 2017 Championships, with the Australian admitting he had been 'bored' during his first-round, straight-sets defeat.

MIXED SINGLES

The tennis authorities hadn't wanted Renée Richards to play in the women's singles at the 1977 US Open. But the New York Supreme Court ruled in her favour and against the United States Tennis Association, and so Richards became the first transsexual to compete at a Grand Slam. She had previously played in the men's singles between 1953 and 1960, when she was Richard Raskind. Unfortunately for Richards, she lost in the opening round to Virginia Wade, who had won that summer's Wimbledon title.

MODELS ON THE BALL

Spain's Secretary of Equality was highly critical of a tournament in Madrid for using models as ball girls and sent a strongly worded letter of protest to the tournament director, a leading sponsor and the city's mayor.

GO HOME

One of the most astonishing sights of recent times was Nick Kyrgios tanking at a tournament in Shanghai in 2016. That included patting a serve over the net and then walking towards his chair before his opponent, Mischa Zverev, had even played his shot. At one stage, the Australian said to the umpire: 'Can you call time so I can finish this match and go home?' Kyrgios was fined and given a suspension.

BOYCOTT

More than 80 male players, including the defending champion Stan Smith, boycotted the 1973 Wimbledon Championships to protest against the suspension of Niki Pilic.

A NOD AND A WINK

Boris Becker didn't help himself, or his then employer, Novak Djokovic, before the 2015 Wimbledon Championships when he suggested that he illegally coached the Serbian during matches. 'There are moments when he looks up and he needs assurance that he is doing it right. And then we have our ways of telling him that it's good or that it's bad. And then it's up to him to change it.'

LARGEST TELEVISION AUDIENCES AND CROWDS

Tennis can command the attention of huge audiences, whether the fans are watching in the stadium, in a bar or from an armchair at home.

116

The size, in millions, of the Chinese television audience that watched the 2011 French Open women's final, when Li Na of China became the first Asian to win a Grand Slam singles title.

= 1 million

17.3

The size, in millions, of the BBC's audience when Andy Murray defeated Novak Djokovic in the 2013 Wimbledon final. That's roughly the same number that watched Björn Borg and John McEnroe contest the 1980 final.

= 1 million

35,681
The size of the crowd when Kim Clijsters played Serena Williams in an exhibition match in Brussels in 2010.

30,472
The number of spectators who watched the 'Battle of the Sexes' match in Houston in 1973, when Billie Jean King defeated Bobby Riggs.

27,488
The number of spectators who attended one day of the 2014 Davis Cup final in Lille between France and Switzerland, a record for a sanctioned tennis match.

23,771
The capacity of the US Open's Arthur Ashe Stadium.

15,000
The capacity of Wimbledon's Centre Court.

15,000
The capacity of the Australian Open's Rod Laver Arena.

14,911
The capacity of the Philippe–Chatrier Court at Roland Garros, home of the French Open.

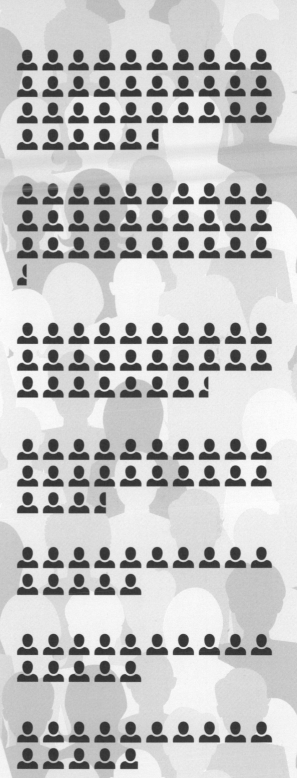

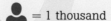 = 1 thousand

DIETS

Some tennis players are extremely careful about what they eat and rarely stray from a strict diet of pasta and chicken breasts. Others are a little more adventurous.

DOG FOOD
Serena Williams once made herself ill by sampling some dog food from a hotel fridge. 'I mean, it did taste weird. … a little bit like a house cleaner kind of thing. I don't know what they put in this dog food,' said Williams, who was in Rome at the time. 'Let's fast-forward two hours – I just ran to the toilet like I was going to pass out.'

CHEGAN
Venus Williams, once a carnivore, has described herself as 'a chegan', which is a vegan who occasionally cheats. 'If you were seated next to me and turned your head for just a second, your meat platter would vanish as if by magic,' she once said. Venus became a vegan after being diagnosed with an autoimmune disease, Sjogren's syndrome.

ANTI-SPANISH
For a Spaniard, Rafael Nadal has some unexpected tastes. As his own mother noted: 'He loathes cheese and tomato and also ham, the national dish of Spain. I'm not as mad about ham myself as most people seem to be, but cheese?'

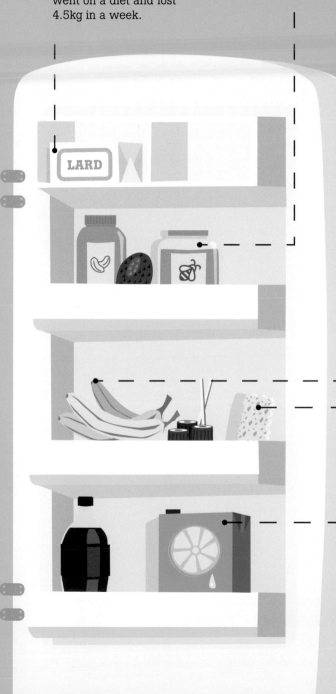

FAT BUSTER
Conscious of his weight in the days leading up to the Australian Open, his home Grand Slam, Bernard Tomic went on a diet and lost 4.5kg in a week.

GLUTEN-FREE
Going gluten-free has only been the half of it for Novak Djokovic, who, on waking, drinks a tall glass of room-temperature water and then eats two spoonfuls of honey. And not just any honey but a specialist sort called manuka honey. His diet now includes plenty of avocados, cashew butter and cups of liquorice tea. One of the foods he has cut out is chocolate, although after winning one Grand Slam he celebrated by breaking off a square of chocolate and placing it on his tongue, just to remind himself what it tasted like.

PATHETIC FRUIT
Andy Murray has expressed some strong views on fruit. 'To be honest, I think bananas are a pathetic fruit.' He is keener on sushi, to the extent that he has been known to eat more than 50 pieces in one sitting.

'Don't try the fried Mars bar' was Andy Murray's advice to Roger Federer before the Swiss player visited Scotland. 'I tried one and it was horrific.'

JUICE OVERLOAD
Patty Schnyder, a former Swiss player, achieved notoriety by drinking up to 3 litres of orange juice a day under the guidance of a man who described himself as 'a natural therapist'. That 'therapist' had some bizarre views, to put it mildly. He once suggested he had found the cure for cancer, and treated Schnyder's sports injuries with hot wax and rolling pins covered in needles.

GREATEST UPSETS

As much as tennis crowds adore the sport's champions and Hollywood names, they also love to see those same players come unstuck against the journeymen and journeywomen of the tour.

	R. VINCI	US OPEN	S. WILLIAMS	
2-6	6-4	6-4		

'This is monumental, it's a shocker, and one of the biggest upsets in the history of tennis,' said Tracy Austin after Serena Williams lost to **Roberta Vinci**, an unseeded Italian, in the semi-finals of the 2015 US Open. Williams had been just two matches away from becoming the first woman since Steffi Graf in 1988 to achieve the calendar-year Grand Slam.

	D. ISTOMIN	US OPEN	N. DJOKOVIC	
7-6	5-7	2-6	7-6	6-4

'First of all, I feel sorry for Novak because I was playing so good today.' So said **Denis Istomin**, a wild card from Uzbekistan ranked 117 in the world, coached by his mother and wearing neon green prescription glasses, after beating Novak Djokovic in the second round of the 2017 Australian Open.

	P. DOOHAN	WIMBLEDON	B. BECKER	
7-6	4-6	6-2	6-4	

'The Becker Wrecker' was the name given to **Peter Doohan**, the Australian who defeated Boris in the second round of the 1987 Wimbledon Championships. Becker had won the 1985 title at the age of 17 and also been the champion the following summer, at 18. But when he was 19, it just wasn't to be for the German. Still, as Becker reminded everyone, this was just a tennis match, not a war, and nobody died.

	L. McNEIL	WIMBLEDON	S. GRAF	
7-5	7-6			

'Steffi Graf, the unstoppable juggernaut of women's tennis, had just been run over by a Lori.' That was the headline in one of the British tabloids the morning after Graf was beaten in the opening round of the 1994 Wimbledon Championships by **Lori McNeil**. Graf had been on a run of three successive titles, or 21 consecutive match victories, on the grass, but that was slashed to zero as she became the first women's defending champion in the tournament's history to lose in the first round.

J. DOKIC	**WIMBLEDON**	M. HINGIS		
6-2	6-0			

The audience 'were clapping for her great shots, not against me' said Martina Hingis, the world number one, after her first-round 1999 Wimbledon defeat to **Jelena Dokic**, a 16-year-old qualifier ranked outside the top 100. Amazingly, Hingis won just two games.

G. BASTL	**WIMBLEDON**	P. SAMPRAS		
6-3	6-2	4-6	3-6	6-4

The 'Graveyard of Champions' was the name given to the old No. 2 Court at Wimbledon, and the biggest burial of all came in the second round of the 2002 Championships when Pete Sampras, winner of seven Wimbledon titles, lost to **George Bastl**, a winner but also a 'lucky loser', who qualified for the main draw only after someone else's late withdrawal.

L. ROSOL	**WIMBLEDON**	R. NADAL		
6-7	6-4	6-4	2-6	6-4

'I'm very, very disappointed [but] it's not a tragedy, it's only a tennis match' was Rafael Nadal's comment after his shock defeat in the second round to **Lukáš Rosol** at Wimbledon in 2012. The way that Rosol struck his forehand – with such power, ambition and accuracy – is still astonishing to recall. At the time, the Czech was ranked only 100 in the world.

S. STAKHOVSKY	**WIMBLEDON**	R. FEDERER	
6-7	7-6	7-5	7-6

Wild Wednesday is how some remember the third day of the 2013 Wimbledon Championships, while others prefer Wacky Wednesday or Wipeout Wednesday on a day of shocks and upsets. The greatest shock of all was **Sergiy Stakhovsky**, a Ukrainian ranked outside the top 100, beating the defending champion, Roger Federer, in the second round.

R. SODERLING	**FRENCH OPEN**	R. NADAL	
6-2	6-7	6-4	7-6

As one observer put it, 'If the Eiffel Tower had suddenly toppled, or the Arc de Triomphe had crumbled into small pieces', it would have been less shocking than what happened on the clay of the 2009 French Open. Until Rafael Nadal played **Robin Soderling** in the fourth round, he was unbeaten in Paris and chasing a fifth consecutive title. And yet somehow Nadal lost to the Swede, whom he had beaten just weeks earlier, also on clay, for the loss of one game.

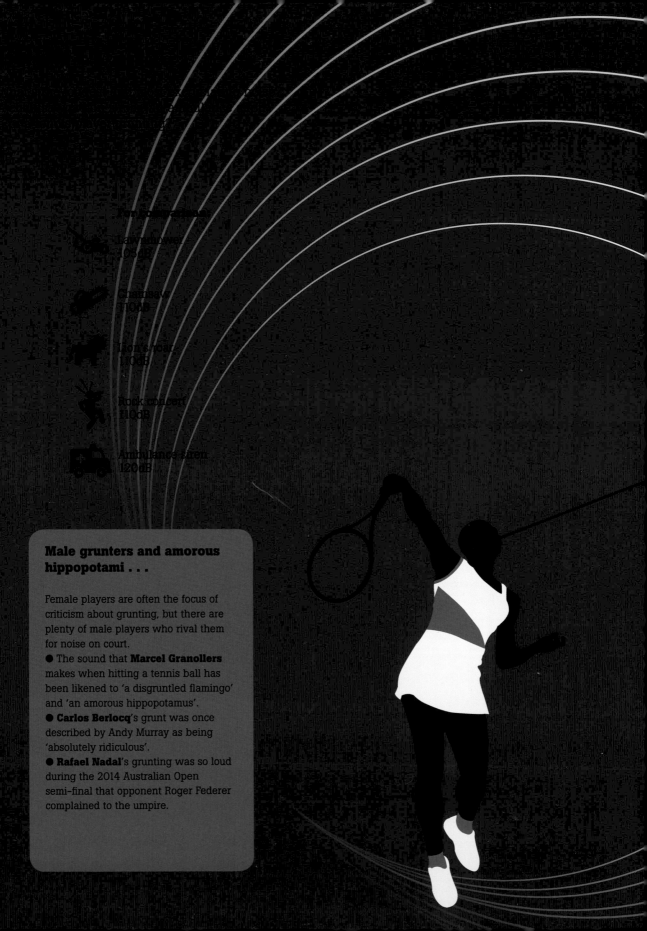

For comparison:

Lawnmower
105dB

Chainsaw
110dB

Lion's roar
110dB

Rock concert
110dB

Ambulance siren
120dB

Male grunters and amorous hippopotami . . .

Female players are often the focus of criticism about grunting, but there are plenty of male players who rival them for noise on court.

● The sound that **Marcel Granollers** makes when hitting a tennis ball has been likened to 'a disgruntled flamingo' and 'an amorous hippopotamus'.

● **Carlos Berlocq**'s grunt was once described by Andy Murray as being 'absolutely ridiculous'.

● **Rafael Nadal**'s grunting was so loud during the 2014 Australian Open semi-final that opponent Roger Federer complained to the umpire.

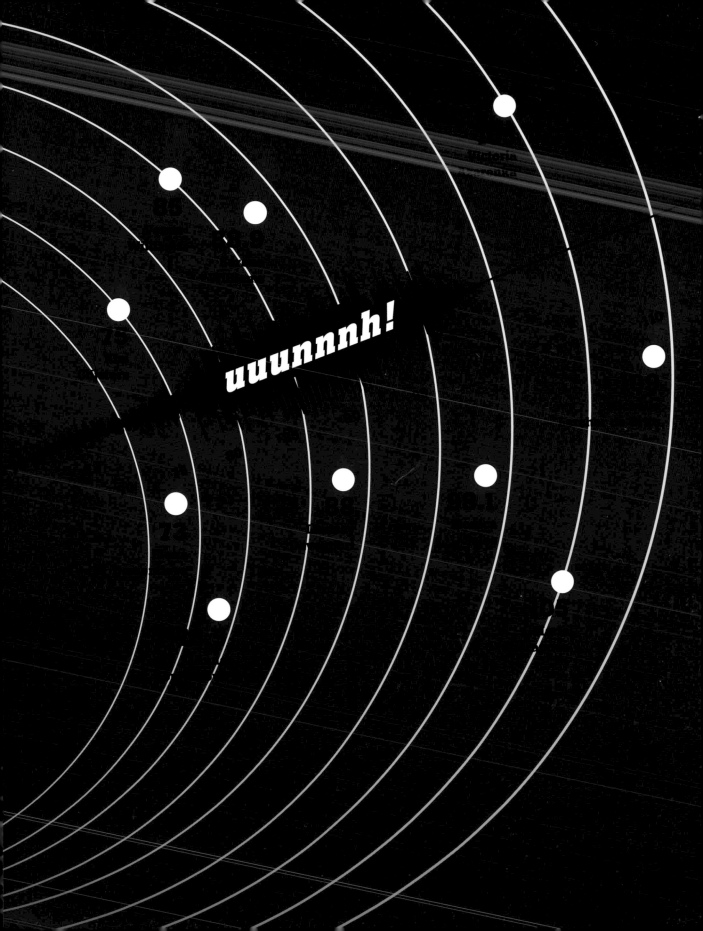

PLAYERS' DOGS

In the volatile, ultra-competitive and often lonely world of professional tennis, a dog can sometimes be the only friend you can rely on.

K.D.

Killer Dog was the name of the hound Martina Navratilova toured the world with. Her pet waited on a pillow in the players' lounge while her owner competed on court.

Andy Murray's dog, Maggie May, is a published author – she wrote a book entitled *How to Look After Your Human: A Dog's Guide* – with a little help from Murray's wife, Kim.

Maria Sharapova's Pomeranian, Dolce, is very strong-willed, according to the Russian: 'He's not a pushover and not afraid to tell you how he feels.'

Playing Wimbledon one summer, Svetlana Kuznetsova had hoped to have her American bulldog, Dolce, with her. Unfortunately, Dolce had to be kept in quarantine. So every day during the tournament, the former Grand Slam champion made the journey from Wimbledon to the facility near Heathrow airport. 'I was crying so much,' she has recalled.

Novak Djokovic's poodle, Pierre, once flirted with Andy Murray's border terrier, Maggie May, on Twitter (or was that just their owners being silly?). In a rare coup for a dog, Pierre has appeared on the front cover of *Vogue* magazine. Djokovic has another dog, Tesla, who is named after Nikola Tesla, a Serbian–American inventor who believed he could create a death-ray that would 'melt' aeroplane motors at a distance of 250 miles.

Venus Williams said that Harold, a Havanese, stopped her from feeling lonely on the tour. 'You're out there on your own and you need a friend who's there for you – after wins or losses – and who really cares for you. I found that someone, and that's Harold. Whether I win or lose, Harold doesn't even know. He doesn't even like tennis. He just waits for me to get off the court.'

ICON JIMMY CONNORS

One of the most combative and controversial figures to have ever gripped a racket, Connors was the antidote to suggestions that tennis was a 'soft' sport.

THE FACTS

NICKNAME
The Brash Basher
of Belleville

DATE OF BIRTH
2 September 1952

BIRTHPLACE
East St Louis,
United States

HEIGHT
1.77m (5ft 10in)

PLAYING STYLE
Left-handed (two-handed
backhand)

3

Connors is the only player to have won the US Open on all three different surfaces – grass, hard and clay.

RECORDS

109
Connors has won more singles titles than any other man.

1,535
The most singles appearances.

1,256
Connors also holds the record for the most singles match wins.

5
He was the first man to win five US Open titles, although Pete Sampras and Roger Federer have since equalled that record.

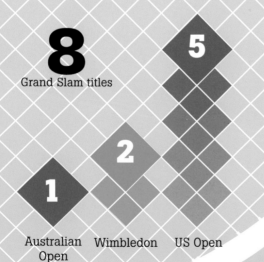

8
Grand Slam titles

5

2

1

Australian Open   Wimbledon   US Open

CONNORS
IN NUMBERS

1988
The year that Connors auditioned to be the host of the US gameshow *Wheel of Fortune.* He didn't get the job.

1
Connors had coached Maria Sharapova for just one match when she ended the partnership.

4
The number of times he reached the semi-finals of the French Open, the only major that eluded him.

39
Connors' age when he made the semi-finals of the 1991 US Open. That was his last great run and there was no schmaltzy ending. 'I wasn't interested in some grand, dumb-ass farewell tour, even though … it would have been worth a small fortune.'

3
The number of hip operations Connors has had.

CELEBRITY TENNIS FANS

From Trump to Tyson, which famous faces are known for their love of the sport?

Sachin Tendulkar is one of the greatest ever cricketers. But, as a boy, he wanted to be John McEnroe. 'I love McEnroe. They would call me Mac because, while everyone else liked Björn Borg, I was crazy about McEnroe. I tried wearing headbands and sweatbands and whooping at people. It didn't quite work.'

When he was a reality television performer rather than US president, Donald Trump was a regular at the US Open. Nick Kyrgios was less of a fan – he was spotted around the time of Trump's inauguration in 2017 wearing a T-shirt which had a four-letter word for Trump and showed 'The Donald' with devil horns.

Anna Wintour, the editor-in-chief of American *Vogue*, is one of the most formidable figures in the fashion industry. But she does have a softer side, which comes out when she is watching her beloved Roger Federer play. During Federer's matches at Grand Slams, Wintour can often be found in Federer's guest box. Away from the court, she has hosted a birthday party for Federer in Manhattan, sent him suits she has picked out and invited him to sit with her on the front row of fashion shows.

The Duchess of Cambridge replaced Queen Elizabeth II as the patron of the All England Club. And, unlike the Queen, she has a genuine interest in the sport. Roger Federer and his wife, Mirka, were once lunch guests at the home of the Duchess's parents in the English countryside. Her husband, the Duke, is also interested in the sport, but she's the biggest racket-head in the royal family.

Such is golf legend Jack Nicklaus's love of tennis that he has grass courts in the garden of his Florida home, on which Serena Williams has trained in preparation for Wimbledon.

Actor Bradley Cooper's adoration for Roger Federer is so great that he has been spotted wearing an 'RF' cap while sitting in Federer's courtside box.

James Bond made a memorable intervention at the 2012 US Open, where Andy Murray scored his first Grand Slam title. Sir Sean Connery burst into Murray's press conference that followed his semi-final victory, with the actor accompanied by Sir Alex Ferguson, the former Manchester United manager, and Judy, the player's mother. Murray said to his mother: 'You smell of wine.' She blamed Connery: 'He made me have wine.'

Former boxer Mike Tyson admires 'the passion' of elite tennis players. 'These are all apex athletes, the best in the universe. You're not going to find better than these.'

Andy Murray once described Will Ferrell as his 'favourite comedian' and so the Briton was amused, rather than upset, when the American mocked his dress sense during a live television interview at the US Open one summer. Ferrell was particularly rude about Murray's red sneakers. Another year in New York, Ferrell flexed his bicep from the stands, mimicking Murray's celebration from earlier that summer at Wimbledon.

Is Beyoncé a tennis fan or just a Serena Williams fan? Accompanied by her husband, Jay-Z, the singer has supported Williams at the Grand Slams. To reciprocate, Williams appeared in one of Beyoncé's music videos.

LEFT-HANDED CHAMPIONS

Have left-handed players won a disproportionately large number of Grand Slams? And which right-handed champion could possibly have won multiple majors with her left hand?

Estimated percentage of the world's population that is left-handed.

10

Percentage of singles titles won by left-handed players during the Open era, which began in 1968.

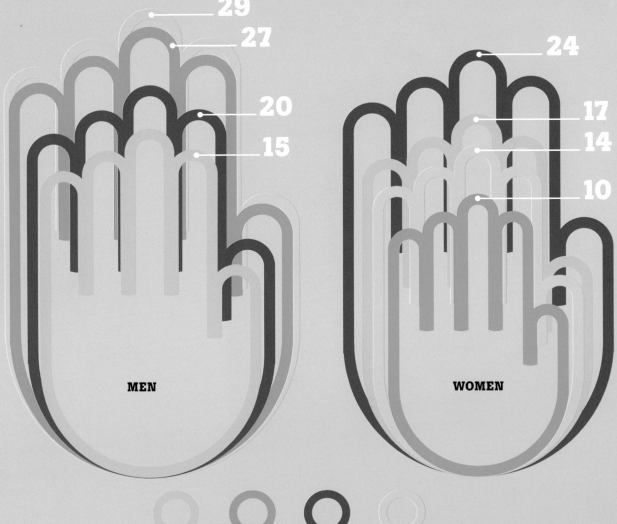

29
27
20
15

MEN

24
17
14
10

WOMEN

Australian Open   **French Open**   **Wimbledon**   **US Open**

4.34a.m. The latest finish to a Grand Slam match, when **Lleyton Hewitt** beat **Marcos Baghdatis** in the third round of the 2008 Australian Open.

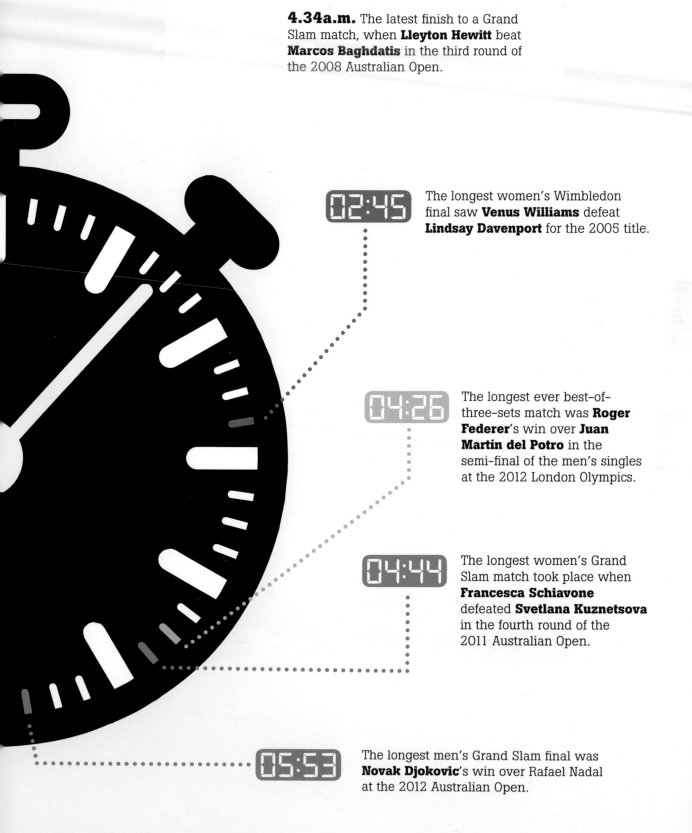

02:45 The longest women's Wimbledon final saw **Venus Williams** defeat **Lindsay Davenport** for the 2005 title.

04:26 The longest ever best-of-three-sets match was **Roger Federer**'s win over **Juan Martin del Potro** in the semi-final of the men's singles at the 2012 London Olympics.

04:44 The longest women's Grand Slam match took place when **Francesca Schiavone** defeated **Svetlana Kuznetsova** in the fourth round of the 2011 Australian Open.

05:53 The longest men's Grand Slam final was **Novak Djokovic**'s win over Rafael Nadal at the 2012 Australian Open.

ICON ANDY MURRAY

The greatest British tennis player of all time, Sir Andrew Barron Murray is also the first active tennis knight (Fred Perry, by contrast, was just a plain Mister).

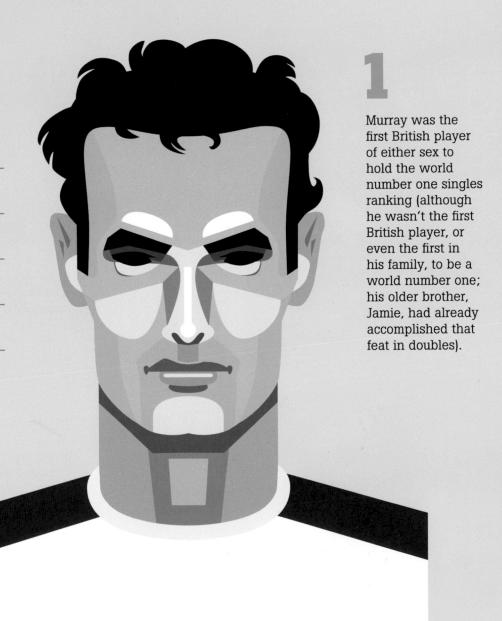

THE FACTS

NICKNAME
Muzza

DATE OF BIRTH
15 May 1987

BIRTHPLACE
Glasgow, Scotland

HEIGHT
1.91m (6ft 3in)

PLAYING STYLE
Right-handed (two-handed backhand)

1

Murray was the first British player of either sex to hold the world number one singles ranking (although he wasn't the first British player, or even the first in his family, to be a world number one; his older brother, Jamie, had already accomplished that feat in doubles).

RECORDS

77

By winning the 2013 Wimbledon title, Murray became the first British men's singles champion at the All England Club for 77 years.

2

Murray became the first player of either sex to win two consecutive Olympic singles gold medals, with his victories in London in 2012 and Rio de Janeiro in 2016.

3

In 2016, Murray became the first person to win the BBC Sports Personality of the Year award for the third time.

3

Grand Slam titles

Wimbledon — 2

US Open — 1

MURRAY IN NUMBERS

1

He is the first active tennis player to be knighted. The only other tennis playing knight of the realm was Sir Norman Brookes, but the Australian didn't receive that honour until after retirement.

76

With his triumph at the 2012 US Open, Murray became the first British man to win a Grand Slam singles title for 76 years.

4

Murray lost his first four Grand Slam singles finals, as did his coach Ivan Lendl, who went on to score eight majors.

1

Over the years, Murray has been in the unfortunate habit of shouting at his coaches. There's only one coach he has never screamed at during a match, and that's Lendl.

79

When Murray propelled Great Britain to victory in the 2015 Davis Cup, by beating Belgium in Ghent, it ended a 79-year wait for victory in the competition.

1

When Murray linked up with Amélie Mauresmo, he became the first leading male player of his generation to work with a female coach.

TATTOOS

Tennis may have had its beginnings on vicars' lawns, and Wimbledon still styles itself as an English summer garden party, but that hasn't stopped many of the world's leading players from visiting the tattoo parlour.

DAN EVANS

The rascal of British tennis has an Oscar Wilde quote tattooed on to his skin: 'Every saint has a past, every sinner has a future'. He also has a tattoo of Jesus.

BORNA ĆORIĆ

The ambitious young Croatian has these bold words on his bicep: 'There's nothing worse in this life than being ordinary'.

MARK PHILIPPOUSSIS

An Australian of Greek heritage, the former Grand Slam finalist has a tattoo of Alexander the Great on his shoulder.

JANKO TIPSAREVIĆ

The Serbian, who was once ranked in the world top 10, is one of the best-read players, and has a line from Dostoyevsky's *The Idiot* as a tattoo: 'Beauty will save the world'.

Ever tried. Ever failed. No matter. Try again. Fail again. Fail better.

STAN WAWRINKA

The Swiss player has a Samuel Beckett quote inked on to his arm, that articulates his philosophy on life and tennis.

AMÉLIE MAURESMO

The former Grand Slam champion, and Andy Murray's ex-coach, has an angel design on her shoulder.

LUKÁŠ ROSOL

Best known for his second-round victory over Rafael Nadal in the second round of the 2012 Wimbledon Championships, one of the greatest upsets in the tournament's history, the Czech has another way of showing his warrior spirit – a large Maori tattoo on his leg.

ANNA KOURNIKOVA

The Russian's lower back is decorated with a sun design.

SVETLANA KUZNETSOVA

The former French Open and US Open champion demonstrates her uncompromising approach with these words tattooed on her bicep: 'Pain doesn't kill me – I kill the pain'. That's not the only inscription on her body, with another tattoo reading: 'Only God is our judge'. She also has a star on her arm, a motif on her chest, and her parents' and grandparents' initials tattooed on to her left hand.

LAURA ROBSON

The former junior Wimbledon champion has a star tattoo on her torso.

BETHANIE MATTEK-SANDS

The American has the most colourful of all the designs in tennis – her right arm is covered in a tattoo that incorporates flowers and bees.

SERENA WILLIAMS

The multiple Grand Slam winner has some discreet tattoos – a rose on her shoulder and a heart on her neck.

GAËL MONFILS

The Frenchman, who likes to be airborne when playing, often diving across the court, has large wings tattooed on to his lower back.

WIMBLEDON IN NUMBERS

The oldest of the four Grand Slams, Wimbledon would be nothing without its traditions. Not just the strawberries and the almost-all-white clothing rules, but also those started by the players, such as pinching the towels.

The time – 2 a.m. – that the head groundsman wakes some mornings, worried about foxes urinating on the Centre Court grass. The chemicals in the urine can burn through the grass, leaving holes the size of dinner plates.

The time – 6 a.m. – that those queuing overnight for tickets are woken up by the stewards so they can take down their tents and clear away any other camping equipment. This is to make space for those arriving later.

The year that the first men's singles competition was held, with the inaugural champion, Spencer Gore, predicting that tennis would never catch on: 'Lawn tennis will never rank among our great games'. One of the motivations for holding that tournament had been to raise funds for a roller to maintain the club's croquet lawns.

1877

1884

The year that a women's singles competition was first held, much to the annoyance of some traditionalists, who feared that female players would become 'attractions' providing 'entertainment'. One grandee said that the 'unblushing' women were taking part in activities that their grandmothers would have regarded as 'unalloyed heathenism'.

1997

The year that the All England Club first used the underground tunnels for those crossing the grounds. To avoid the crowds, the players regularly use the tunnels to walk from the practice courts to the locker room.

10

The maximum width, in millimetres, of the colour trim allowed on shirts and tops, which must otherwise be white. The same measurement also applies to shorts, skirts, tracksuit bottoms, caps, headbands, bandanas, wristbands, socks and undergarments.

90

Clothing manufacturers are expected to send the players' outfits to the All England Club at least 90 days before the start of the fortnight to ensure they adhere to the strict almost-all-white clothing rules.

The approximate value, in pounds, of the towels taken by players at every year's Championships – around 4,000 towels, costing about £30 each. To deter the juniors, the All England Club gives them plain white towels rather than ones with any colour or branding.

120,000

170,000

The approximate number of glasses of Pimm's drunk in the fortnight.

28

The weight, in tonnes, of strawberries consumed during the tournament. To ensure the fruit is fresh, the berries are picked at 4 a.m. each day and then transported from a farm in Kent.

2,700

The weight, in kilograms, of the bananas eaten by the players over the fortnight.

130,000

The approximate number of English scones eaten every Championships.

8

The playing height of the grass – in millimetres – with the lawns cut at 7.30 a.m. every morning of the Championships.

2015

The year that Novak Djokovic and Serena Williams revived the practice of the two singles champions dancing together at the end-of-tournament dinner. This hadn't happened for decades, but Djokovic and Williams put on a slick performance to 'Night Fever', the Bee Gees' disco hit from the film *Saturday Night Fever*.

The cost, in pounds, of buying two tickets for the 2013 men's final between Andy Murray and Novak Djokovic on an online booking website.

83,000

SLAM STADIUMS

History is made each year inside the four Grand Slams' centre courts. Here are some of their statistics, including how long it takes each roof to close.

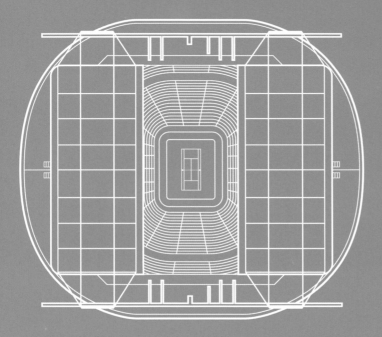

Rod Laver Arena – Australian Open
Capacity: 15,000
Opened: 1988
Cost: 94 million Australian dollars
Surface: Plexicushion
Time it takes for the roof to close:
20 minutes. It is sometimes closed because of extreme heat as well as to protect players from rain.

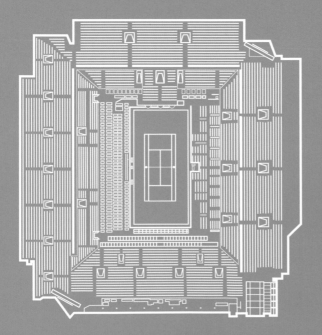

Court Philippe-Chatrier – French Open
Capacity: 14,991
Opened: 1928
Cost: Unknown
Surface: Clay
Roof: The only one of the Grand Slam centre courts without a sliding roof, although the French Tennis Federation hopes to build one that would close in around 15 minutes.

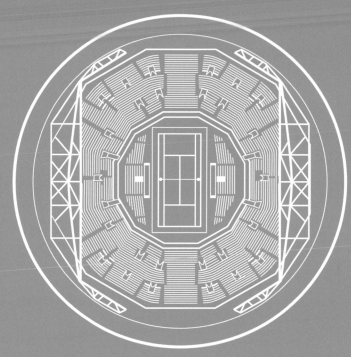

Centre Court – Wimbledon
Capacity: 15,000
Opened: 1922
Cost: The initial costs are unknown. The cost of the roof, which was operational from 2009, has been estimated at 100 million pounds.
Surface: Grass
Time it takes for the roof to close:
8–10 minutes and then a further delay of 20–30 minutes before the air-management system has created the correct playing conditions. Can be used in wind speeds of up to 69kph (43mph).

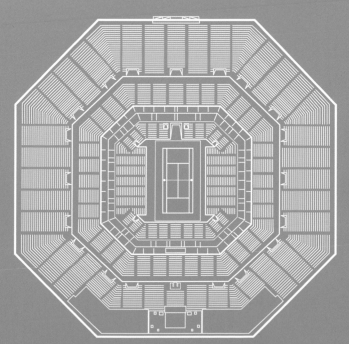

Arthur Ashe Stadium – US Open
Capacity: 23,771
Opened: 1997
Cost: 254 million US dollars initial building cost, plus an estimated bill of 150 million US dollars for the retractable roof, which was ready from 2016.
Surface: DecoTurf
Time it takes for the roof to close:
7 minutes. Can be used in wind speeds of up to 72kph (45mph).

ICON **CHRIS EVERT**

Known for being calm and cool in even the most intense moments, Evert was at her most formidable on clay, but had the game and mental fortitude to win on any surface.

THE FACTS

NICKNAME
The Ice Maiden

DATE OF BIRTH
21 December 1954

BIRTHPLACE
Fort Lauderdale,
United States

HEIGHT
1.68m (5ft 6in)

PLAYING STYLE
Right-handed (two-
handed backhand)

The number of consecutive matches Evert won on clay, the longest streak on one surface. During that six-year run, she dropped just eight sets. Over her career, Evert won almost 95 per cent of her matches on clay.

RECORDS

7

No woman has won more French Open singles titles (and until Rafael Nadal, no man had either).

90

Her career winning percentage of 90 is a record for both sexes.

6

Evert won a record six US Open singles titles – a figure also reached by Serena Williams in 2014.

EVERT
IN NUMBERS

13

The number of consecutive years that Evert won at least one Grand Slam singles title, a run of success that stretched from 1974 to 1986.

55

The number of consecutive wins she achieved in 1974, a record at the time.

157

The singles titles Evert won during her career, second only to Martina Navratilova's 167.

299

The number of Grand Slam singles matches Evert won, a figure only bettered by Serena Williams and Martina Navratilova.

1 million

Evert was the first female tennis player to win one million US dollars in prize money. By the end of her career, she had amassed almost nine million dollars.

18

Grand Slam titles

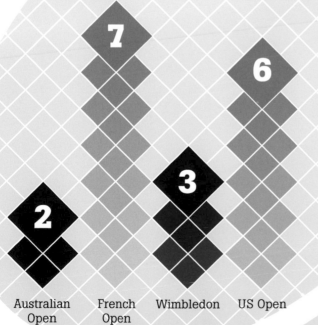

7 French Open

6 US Open

2 Australian Open

3 Wimbledon

FASTEST BACKHANDS

Which men and women players have the biggest backhand?
The numbers here are averages according to data published
by Tennis Australia's Game Insight Group.

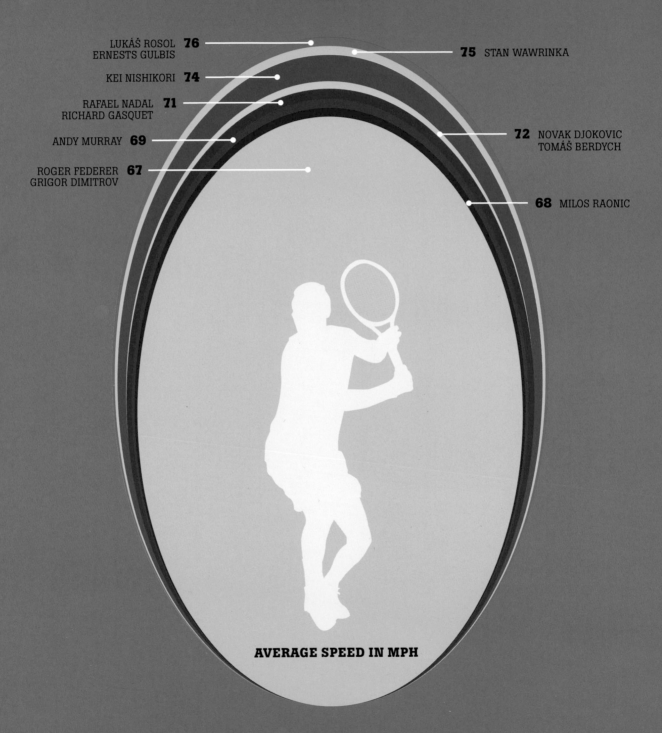

MEN

LUKÁŠ ROSOL **76**
ERNESTS GULBIS

75 STAN WAWRINKA

KEI NISHIKORI **74**

RAFAEL NADAL **71**
RICHARD GASQUET

72 NOVAK DJOKOVIC
TOMÁŠ BERDYCH

ANDY MURRAY **69**

ROGER FEDERER **67**
GRIGOR DIMITROV

68 MILOS RAONIC

AVERAGE SPEED IN MPH

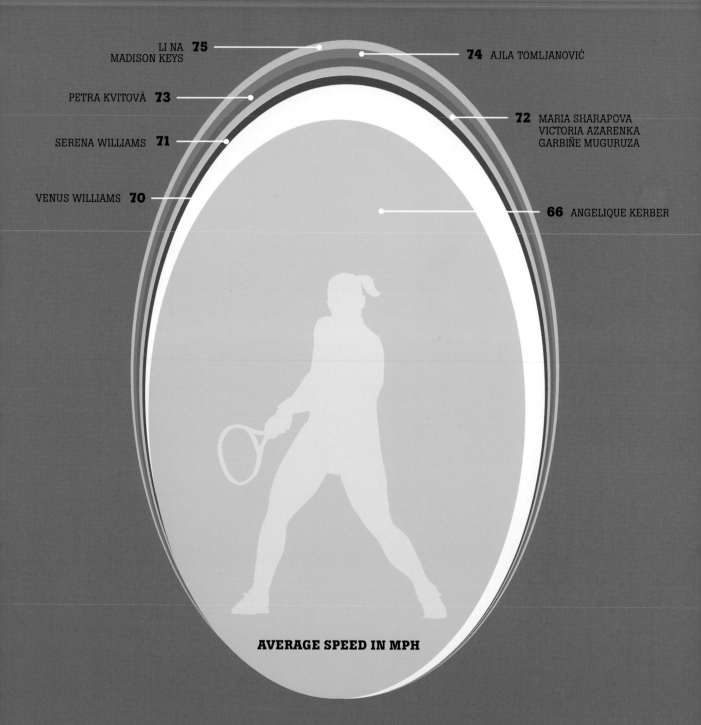

WOMEN

LI NA **75**
MADISON KEYS

74 AJLA TOMLJANOVIĆ

PETRA KVITOVÁ **73**

72 MARIA SHARAPOVA
VICTORIA AZARENKA
GARBIÑE MUGURUZA

SERENA WILLIAMS **71**

VENUS WILLIAMS **70**

66 ANGELIQUE KERBER

AVERAGE SPEED IN MPH

PRIVATE JETS AND OTHER INTERNATIONAL TRAVEL

You can't be a professional tennis player without spending a lot of time on planes. The elite, though, can afford to travel on private jets.

Approximate cost for 25 hours' flying time on a private jet.

£100,000

90,000
The estimated number of air miles per year for a top-10 player on the men's or women's tour.

20
The average number of events played each year by a male or female top-10 tennis player.

55
The number of hours it took Agnieszka Radwańska, a former Wimbledon finalist, to travel from a tournament in Montreal to the Rio Olympics. She then lost her first-round match in just 99 minutes.

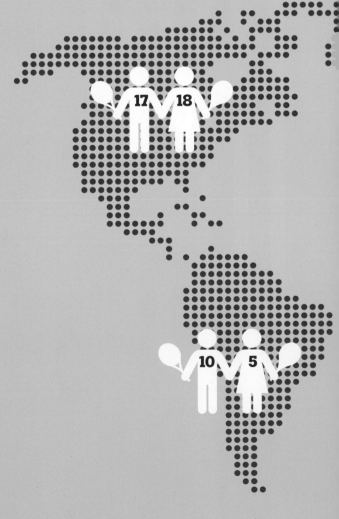

PRIVATE JETS

● Roger Federer, Andy Murray, Novak Djokovic, Rafael Nadal, Serena Williams and **Maria Sharapova** have all used private jets.

● **Federer** has described his jet as a noisy, chaotic place: 'My jet's full. You don't want to be on a jet with my kids, you know.'

● 'One of my greatest luxuries is flying privately,' **Sharapova** has said. 'It really helps me to get to or from a tournament quickly when I have to. It's one of the best investments of my career.'

● Rumours once circulated in tennis that **Ernests Gulbis**, whose father is believed to be one of the richest men in Latvia, travelled between tournaments by private jet. 'Yes,' he said by way of response, 'and I have a helicopter, a submarine and a spaceship.'

PERCENTAGE OF TOURNAMENTS IN EACH CONTINENT

54 40

11 25

2 2

6 10

DRUGS IN TENNIS

Some players have tested positive for performance-enhancing drugs, others for recreational substances, and one even got into trouble for taking a treatment that was supposed to stop him from going bald.

The first year that Pat Cash played Wimbledon, he would keep a joint under his pillow and 'have a smoke every night'. 'It calmed me down. The problem is that you think: "Drugs are supposed to be bad, but that smoke didn't ruin my game." So you take more. Then you take the next drug and the next drug.'

When Maria Sharapova said she would be making 'a major announcement' in March 2016, it was widely assumed she was going to retire, but there was a surprise. 'I know many of you thought I would be retiring today. If I was going to announce my retirement today, it would probably not be in a downtown Los Angeles hotel with this fairly ugly carpet.' In fact, she was using that 'ugly' setting to admit that she had tested positive for a banned substance, meldonium, during that year's Australian Open. She ended up serving a 15-month ban.

Rafael Nadal was awarded damages after a former French sports minister suggested that the Spaniard's long absence from the tour in 2012 wasn't because of injury but because he had failed a drugs test. 'I intend not only to defend my integrity and my image as an athlete, but also the values I have defended all my career.'

Richard Gasquet's French kisses in a Miami nightclub with a woman only ever identified as 'Pamela' caused him untold trouble. The very next day, he tested positive for cocaine. However, he was eventually allowed to continue with his career after the Court of Arbitration for Sport accepted his explanation that he had inadvertently ingested the drug from that close encounter with 'Pamela'.

Of all the explanations that tennis players have offered for positive drugs tests, none can top that given by Petr Korda after a sample he provided one year at Wimbledon was found to contain a banned steroid. Korda blamed his appetite for veal, saying the calves had been fattened-up with injections of nandrolone and that the drug had subsequently built up in his system. That wasn't accepted – scientists calculated that he would have needed to eat 40 calves a day to send the steriod levels that high.

Snorting a line of crystal meth made Andre Agassi want to clean his home. 'I've never felt so alive, so hopeful, and I've never felt such energy. I'm seized by a desperate desire to clean. I go tearing around my house, cleaning it from top to bottom. I dust the furniture. I scour the tub. I make the beds,' said Agassi, who tested positive for the drug, but avoided a ban by saying he had sipped from a drink that had been spiked by his personal assistant.

When Sesil Karatantcheva tested positive for a banned steroid, the Bulgarian teenager claimed that the high levels of nandrolone in her system had been caused by a pregnancy. She was given a two-year ban.

For all his talent and success – he won the 1977 Australian Open – Vitas Gerulaitis was best known for his adventures off the court. An owner of a banana-yellow Rolls-Royce, a friend of Andy Warhol and a regular in the Studio 54 nightclub in Manhattan, Gerulaitis lived a life of excess. He was named in a federal grand jury investigation into drug dealing, though he was subsequently cleared of any wrongdoing. His premature death, at the age of just 40, was attributed to accidental carbon monoxide poisoning.

Such was Boris Becker's dependence on sleeping pills that, after taking a heavy dose in the night, he was half asleep during a Wimbledon final. 'I started the match like a sleepwalker,' Becker said of his defeat to Stefan Edberg in 1990.

A fear of baldness led Mariano Hood, an Argentine doubles player, to fail a doping test – to prevent hair loss, he had been taking a treatment that contained a prohibited substance.

Yannick Noah, a former French Open champion, admitted to smoking marijuana before matches.

SLAMMED

Winning a Grand Slam is the ultimate for any tennis player. These are the men and women who have won the most majors, whether in the amateur or Open eras.

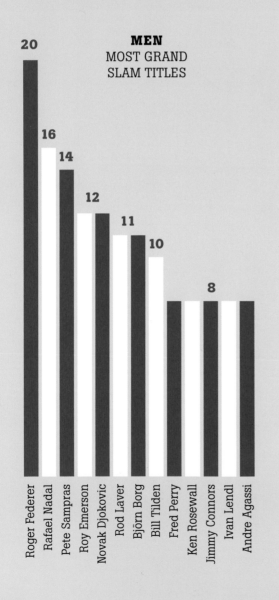

MEN
MOST GRAND
SLAM TITLES

Roger Federer — 20
Rafael Nadal — 16
Pete Sampras — 14
Roy Emerson — 12
Novak Djokovic — 12
Rod Laver — 11
Björn Borg — 11
Bill Tilden — 10
Fred Perry — 8
Ken Rosewall — 8
Jimmy Connors — 8
Ivan Lendl — 8
Andre Agassi — 8

20
5 6
1
8
ROGER FEDERER

16
3 1
2
10
RAFAEL NADAL

14
2
5
7
PETE SAMPRAS

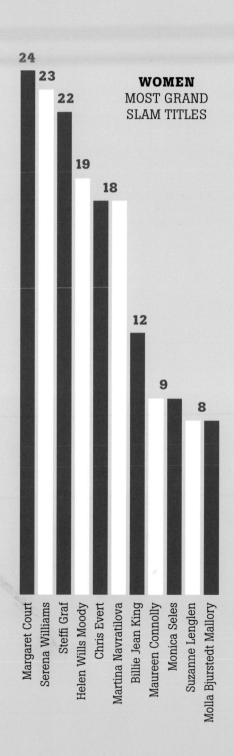

- Australian Open titles
- French Open titles
- Wimbledon titles
- US Open titles

WOMEN
MOST GRAND
SLAM TITLES

24 — Margaret Court
23 — Serena Williams
22 — Steffi Graf
19 — Helen Wills Moody
18 — Chris Evert
18 — Martina Navratilova
12 — Billie Jean King
9 — Maureen Connolly
9 — Monica Seles
8 — Suzanne Lenglen
8 — Molla Bjurstedt Mallory

24

5
3
11
5

MARGARET COURT

23

6
7
7
3

SERENA WILLIAMS

22

5
4
7
6

STEFFI GRAF

BLACK CHAMPIONS

Serena and Venus Williams aren't just astonishing tennis champions; they are also black icons who transcend the sport. The same could be said of the pioneering Althea Gibson, as well as Arthur Ashe and Yannick Noah.

ARTHUR ASHE

Born in Richmond, Virginia – which had been the capital of the pro-slavery confederacy during the American Civil War – Ashe was the first black man to win the US Open. That victory came in 1968 when he was a lieutenant in the army. Two years later, he became the first black men's singles winner at the Australian Open. But perhaps his most memorable victory of all was his Wimbledon triumph in 1975, when he defeated Jimmy Connors to become the first black champion to win on the lawns of the All England Club. Connors had been considered unbeatable, but the night before, during a visit to the Playboy Club, Ashe had settled on the smart tactic of taking the pace off the ball and giving Connors nothing to play with.

YANNICK NOAH

With his victory at the 1983 French Open, Noah became the first black man to win the singles title at the clay-court Grand Slam (he also remains the last Frenchman to have won that tournament). Noah was talent-spotted as a young boy by Arthur Ashe during the American player's tour of Africa – Ashe suggested that Noah move from Cameroon to France to train.

ALTHEA GIBSON

Venus Williams has said how Gibson, the first black icon of the women's game, 'paved the way'. It was at the 1956 French Open that Gibson became the first black woman, as well as the first black player of either sex, to win a Grand Slam singles title. She was also the first black Wimbledon champion, a title she won in 1957 and then retained the following summer. As Billie Jean King said of Gibson's first Centre Court triumph: 'To have an African-American winning Wimbledon in the mid-1950s and having the Queen of England present the trophy on Centre Court, it had to be joyous.'

SERENA AND VENUS WILLIAMS

Their father and first coach, Richard, once spoke of his daughters being the 'ghetto Cinderellas' of the 'lily-white tennis world'. As Serena has said: 'Two black girls from Compton [in Los Angeles] were probably not supposed to play tennis, let alone be any good at it.' Both have held the world number one ranking, and won multiple Grand Slam singles titles. And when Serena won her 23rd major, at the 2017 Australian Open, she became the most successful player, man or woman, of the Open era.

GLASSES, HATS AND HEADPHONES

From headphones to glasses, bandanas to baseball caps, some players know how to accessorise. But which player wanted something 'a bit rock n' roll' to wear on court?

GLASSES

Jaroslav Drobný,
The Czech-born 1954 Wimbledon men's singles champion wore tinted prescription glasses because of an old ice-hockey injury. He is believed to be the only man to have won the Wimbledon title in glasses.

Billie Jean King
In the summer of 1966, King became the first woman to win the Wimbledon singles title while wearing glasses.

Martina Navratilova
A puzzlingly poor start to the 1985 season was soon sorted out once Navratilova realised she needed glasses.

Arthur Ashe
The American wore spectacles while winning the 1968 US Open and the 1970 Australian Open. He later switched to contact lenses after he lost a match in drizzle with steamed-up glasses. In his contacts, he saw the ball well enough to win the 1975 Wimbledon title.

HEADPHONES

HATS

Nick Kyrgios
The Australian is just one of a number of top players who have worn headphones when walking out on court, including Serena Williams, Victoria Azarenka and Dustin Brown.

Pat Cash
The 1987 Wimbledon champion wanted something 'a bit rock n' roll' to wear on court, to make him look like a cross between a tennis player and a guitarist from Guns N' Roses. And that's how Cash came to wear a black and white, checked headband.

John McEnroe
The bandana or headband has been the head gear of choice for McEnroe and many others, such as Björn Borg, Rafael Nadal, Roger Federer, Suzanne Lenglen, Guillermo Vilas, Steffi Graf, Andre Agassi, Gabriela Sabatini, Jana Novotná Juan Martín del Potro and Serena Williams.

Jim Courier
The baseball cap has been a favourite of Americans Courier, Andy Roddick and Andre Agassi, but also of Australian Lleyton Hewitt (backwards) and Briton Andy Murray.

ICON ANDRE AGASSI

As much as Agassi came to loathe the tagline for his Canon advertising campaign – 'Image is Everything' – there can be no doubt that he was one of the most original tennis players in history, as well as one of the most successful.

THE FACTS

NICKNAME
Double A

DATE OF BIRTH
29 April 1970

BIRTHPLACE
Las Vegas, United States

HEIGHT
1.80m (5ft 11in)

PLAYING STYLE
Right-handed (two-handed backhand)

141

Agassi's lowest ranking during his mid-career slump in 1997.

5

Agassi and his wife, Steffi Graf, both have the clean sweep of all four major championship titles and an Olympic gold medal.

RECORDS

1
The Las Vegan was the first man to win all the majors, an Olympic gold medal, the Davis Cup and the season-ending ATP Finals – this is now called the 'Agassi Slam'.

33
Agassi is the oldest man to have held the world number one ranking – he did so in 2003 at the age of 33.

5
At the 1999 French Open, Agassi became only the fifth man to achieve the Career Grand Slam. He was the first to do so on three different surfaces – grass, hard and clay. The previous four men had won their majors on just grass and clay.

4

8
Grand Slam titles

1
1
2

Australian Open | French Open | Wimbledon | US Open

AGASSI
IN NUMBERS

3
The number of consecutive years Agassi skipped Wimbledon, from 1988 to 1990, in part because he didn't like playing on grass. He also regarded the tournament as stuffy, with its all-white clothing rules preventing him from appearing in his ripped denim and neon outfits. However, Agassi returned in 1991, and then won the title the following year for his first Grand Slam title.

14
The difference between Agassi's portfolio of Grand Slam singles titles and his wife Steffi Graf's collection of majors – she won 22.

2,500
The number of tennis balls he would hit every day as a child, spewed out by a machine under the direction of his father. Agassi came to regard that machine as 'The Dragon'.

20
The pins required to keep his wig, a fake mullet, in place for the 1990 French Open final after it fell apart in the shower the night before. 'I prayed – not for victory, but that my hairpiece would not fall off.' Unsurprisingly, he lost.

ACES AND DOUBLE FAULTS

One is something to be proud of, the other is one to forget.
Who holds the records for the most aces and double faults?

113

Most aces in a men's match
John Isner served 113 during his
first-round victory over Nicolas
Mahut at the 2010 Wimbledon
Championships (Mahut is second
in the all-time list after hitting
103 in the same match).

31

**Most aces in a
women's match**
Kristýna Plíšková smashed 31
during her second-round match
against Monica Puig at the
2016 Australian Open,
but still lost.

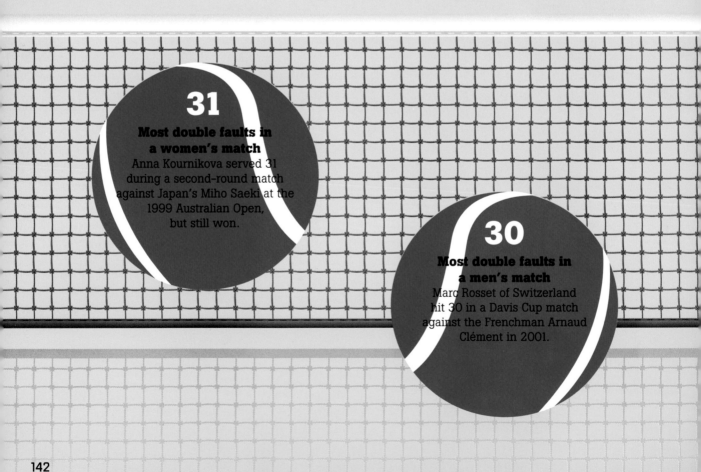

31

**Most double faults in
a women's match**
Anna Kournikova served 31
during a second-round match
against Japan's Miho Saeki at the
1999 Australian Open,
but still won.

30

**Most double faults in
a men's match**
Marc Rosset of Switzerland
hit 30 in a Davis Cup match
against the Frenchman Arnaud
Clément in 2001.

213

Most aces in a men's tournament

Goran Ivanišević served 213 aces on the way to winning the 2001 Wimbledon title.

50

Most aces in a men's Grand Slam final

Roger Federer served 50 aces when beating Andy Roddick for the 2009 Wimbledon title.

102

Most aces in a women's tournament

Serena Williams produced 102 aces during the 2012 Wimbledon Championships.

IVO KARLOVIĆ BY THE NUMBERS

12,302

Over his career, the Croatian has hit more aces than anyone else, after passing Goran Ivanišević's total of 10,131 (figure correct up to end of 2017 season). Ivanišević, though, holds the record for a season, with 1,477 in 1996.

78

The most aces Karlović ever hit in one match was 78, which came during a Davis Cup defeat against Radek Štěpánek of the Czech Republic in 2009 – it remains a high mark for the competition.

75

Karlović holds the record for the most aces in a match at the Australian Open, after smacking 75 past Horacio Zeballos of Argentina in the first round of the 2017 championship.

61

He also has the one-match record at the US Open, with 61 aces against Yen-Hsun Lu in the first round of the 2016 tournament, and for the French Open, where he produced 55 aces during a first-round defeat against Lleyton Hewitt in 2009.

GREATEST CHOKES IN TENNIS HISTORY

Can there be a more excruciating experience for a tennis player than choking on the big stage? Here are five of the biggest on-court disintegrations.

6-3
6-2
4-6
5-7
5-7

CHOKE POINT 1-1 0-30

JOHN McENROE

The American likes to say that anger made him play better tennis. That's not entirely true. Consider what happened in the 1984 French Open final, where he took the opening two sets against Ivan Lendl. McEnroe hadn't lost all year and it didn't look as though that run was going to end anytime soon. But then, noise started leaking out of a cameraman's headset, McEnroe could no longer control himself and the match flipped.

6-0
6-3
4-6
1-6
6-8

CHOKE POINT 4-4 40-0

GUILLERMO CORIA

Before Rafael Nadal, Coria was the King of Clay, and everything appeared to be going to plan for the Argentine in the 2004 French Open final when he won the first two sets against his countryman Gastón Gaudio. Unfortunately for Coria, known as El Mago (The Magician), his game then disappeared in a puff of chalk dust. He complained of cramps, but really this was a mental disintegration. While Coria had a couple of match points in the fifth set, he couldn't convert them, and Gaudio was the unlikeliest of champions.

JANA NOVOTNÁ

The Czech would be rebranded as 'No-No Novotna of Choke-Slovakia' after hitting a double fault that changed the course of a Wimbledon final. Leading 4–1, 40–30 in the third set of the 1993 final against Steffi Graf, Novotná was just five points from victory, but her tennis collapsed after that second serve was called out. 'Novotna was unrecognisable, not an elite player but a beginner again,' the American writer Malcolm Gladwell has noted, and she ended the afternoon sobbing on the Duchess of Kent's shoulder.

CHOKE POINT 4-1 40-30

6-7
6-1
4-6

CHOKE POINT
5-1
30-0

→ **6-1**
6-7
8-10

GABRIELA SABATINI
'A knack for fashioning disaster from a routine victory' was one American writer's assessment of Sabatini's occasional inability to close matches out. The most extraordinary of all her collapses was from 6–1, 5–1 in her 1993 French Open quarter-final against Mary Joe Fernández.

MARTINA HINGIS
It was the Parisian afternoon when, in Hingis's own words, she lost her mind. Leading by a set and a break in the 1999 French Open final against Steffi Graf, the Swiss player relinquished her poise and composure after querying a line call, even breaching protocol by walking around the net to look for a mark on the clay on the German's side of the court. On losing the match, Hingis left the court in tears and had to be persuaded by her mother to return for the trophy ceremony.

CHOKE POINT
2-0
0-15

→ **6-4**
5-7
2-6

'I don't want anybody to talk about my nerves anymore'

AMÉLIE MAURESMO
After developing a reputation as a player prone to choking, Mauresmo felt she had proven herself after beating Justine Henin-Hardenne in the 2006 Wimbledon final. She came from a set down to win the match 2-6, 6-3, 6-4.

GREATEST COACHES

Behind every great player is a great coach.
How are those coaches and players connected?

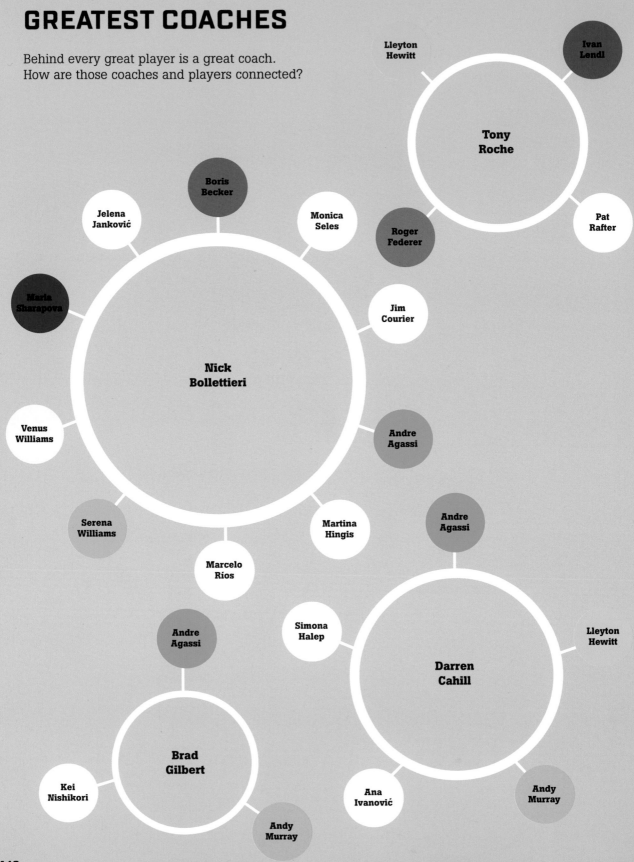

Lleyton Hewitt

Ivan Lendl

Tony Roche

Pat Rafter

Boris Becker

Jelena Janković

Monica Seles

Roger Federer

Maria Sharapova

Jim Courier

Nick Bollettieri

Venus Williams

Andre Agassi

Serena Williams

Martina Hingis

Andre Agassi

Marcelo Ríos

Simona Halep

Lleyton Hewitt

Andre Agassi

Darren Cahill

Brad Gilbert

Kei Nishikori

Ana Ivanović

Andy Murray

Andy Murray

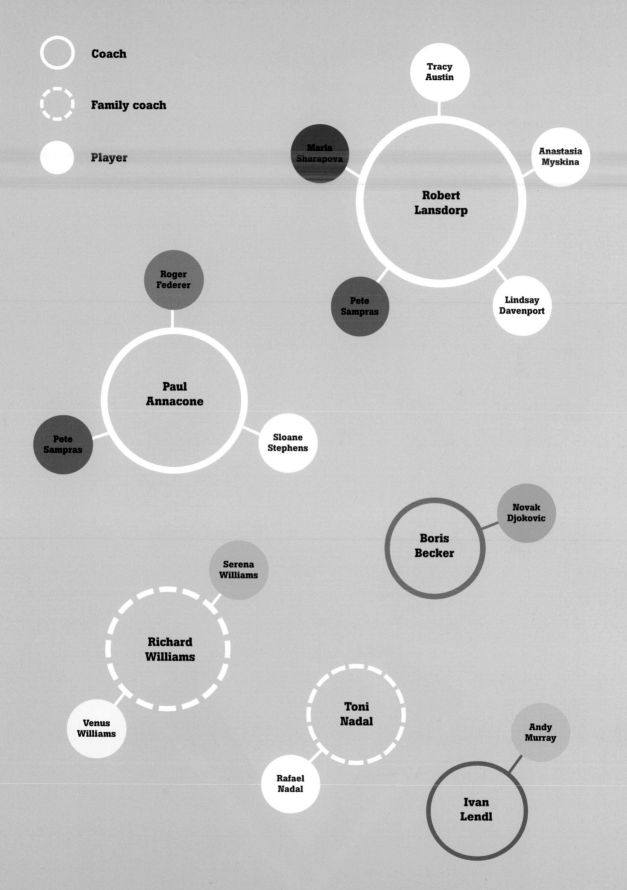

ICON JOHN McENROE

In his prime, McEnroe was much more than an angry young man – he was an extraordinarily gifted tennis player. Anger alone doesn't win you that many Grand Slams.

THE FACTS

NICKNAME
Super Brat

DATE OF BIRTH
16 February 1959

BIRTHPLACE
Wiesbaden, West Germany

HEIGHT
1.80m (5ft 11in)

PLAYING STYLE
Left-handed (one-handed backhand)

17

The total number of major titles – singles, doubles and mixed doubles – won by McEnroe. The first came in 1977 when he played mixed doubles as an amateur with Mary Carillo at the French Open.

RECORDS

96.5

McEnroe's winning percentage in 1984, with 82 victories from 85 matches, which is the highest season-long winning percentage for any man in the Open era.

19

The age at which McEnroe first won the ATP's season-ending tournament. He remains the youngest champion in its history.

1

After winning the title in 1981, McEnroe became the first Wimbledon men's singles champion not to automatically receive membership to the All England Club.

7

Grand Slam titles

3

4

Wimbledon   US Open

McENROE
IN NUMBERS

1

The only time that McEnroe appeared in the French Open final was in 1984. He led Ivan Lendl by two sets to love, but his afternoon unravelled after he was distracted by the noise leaking from a television cameraman's headset.

1

McEnroe was defaulted from a match only once during his career. It happened at the 1990 Australian Open against Sweden's Mikael Pernfors.

1977

The year that, as a teenager, amateur McEnroe played his way through Wimbledon qualifying and then made the semi-finals of the main draw.

1

McEnroe's only appearance in an Australian Open semi-final came in 1983. This was his best result at the tournament, which he played in only five times.

8

After swearing at the chairman's wife on the practice court, McEnroe was banned from Queen's Club in West London and didn't play the pre-Wimbledon event for eight years.

THE WORLD NUMBER ONE

The ranking doesn't lie – reach the top of the list and you're the best tennis player on the planet.

WTA The Women's Tennis Association runs the WTA Tour, the professional women's circuit.

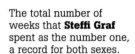

377

The total number of weeks that **Steffi Graf** spent as the number one, a record for both sexes.

4

The number of players to have held the number one ranking who have never won a Grand Slam title – they are **Jelena Janković, Dinara Safina, Karolína Plíšková** and **Simona Halep.**

Serena Williams and **Steffi Graf** share the record for the longest stretch of consecutive weeks at the top of the standings.

186

2

In 2007, **Evonne Goolagong** was informed by the WTA that she had spent two weeks as the number one in 1976. At the time, not all of her ranking points had been entered into the computer so she had missed out on the status and recognition.

The number of years that **Steffi Graf** finished as the number one, also a record.

8

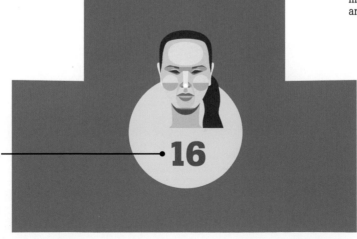

Martina Hingis' age when she first became the alpha female of the women's game, making her the youngest number one in history.

16

150

ATP

ATP The Association of Tennis Professionals runs the ATP World Tour, the professional men's circuit.

302 The total number of weeks **Roger Federer** has spent at the top of the rankings, a record for the men's game.

237 The number of consecutive weeks that **Federer** has held the number one ranking – another record.

6 The number of years that **Pete Sampras** finished as the world number one, which is without parallel (those six years were all consecutive).

1973 The year that the ATP introduced the official rankings, with **Ilie Nastase** the first number one.

26 When **Andy Murray** became the number one in November 2016, he was the 26th man in history to accomplish that ranking.

17 **Murray** was the 17th man to finish one or more seasons as the number one after doing so in 2016 (that accomplishment came through beating Novak Djokovic in a winner-takes-all final of the season-ending ATP Finals in London).

1 The number of weeks that **Pat Rafter** spent as the world number one – no other man has had such a short stay at the tennis summit.

20 The age, in years, at which **Lleyton Hewitt** became the number one, making him the youngest in history.

1 The number of weeks, between 1975 and 1976, that some believe **Guillermo Vilas** was the top-ranked player (this was a time when the ranking list wasn't published weekly). However, the ATP declined to retrospectively make him the number one.

1 **Marcelo Ríos** is the only man to have held the number one ranking who never won a Grand Slam.

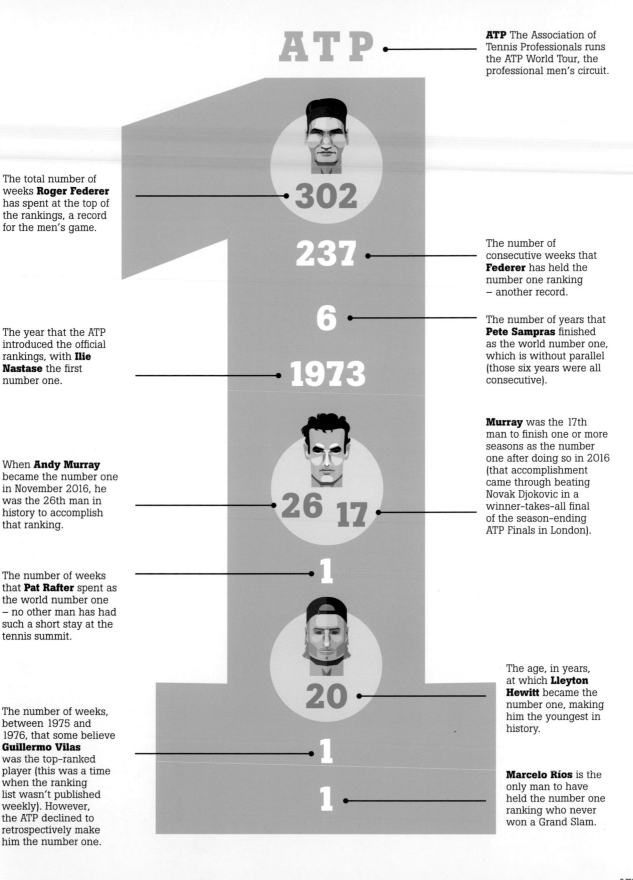

151

SMASHING RACKETS

There are few more thrilling sights on a tennis court than a player smashing a racket to pieces, even if the tennis authorities don't quite see it that way.

x 700 = 💰

MARAT SAFIN

The Russian is remembered as much for destroying rackets as he is for winning Grand Slam singles titles. 'I guess I smashed 700 rackets during my career, maybe more. That's not too many. The rackets cost about $200 each, so 700 rackets at $200, that's not so much, really. That's OK, I think,' said Safin. The overall bill for his destruction would be even higher if you added in all the fines he received.

x 0 = 😠

GORAN IVANIŠEVIC

Winning the 2001 Wimbledon title wasn't the only historical feat that the Croat achieved in England – the season before, he was defaulted from a match in Brighton 'due to lack of appropriate equipment' after breaking all his rackets. 'I was angry,' he explained.

x 70 = 🙁

ERNESTS GULBIS

Breaking as many rackets as Gulbis has – the Latvian has estimated he was destroying up to 70 a year – can lead to feelings of guilt. 'I went to the factory where they made the rackets and I saw all the work they do,' the former French Open semi-finalist confessed. 'The rackets are handmade and they do everything for the players, they really think about what the players need, and then an idiot like me comes along and breaks them. Sorry, those are my emotions and I can't hide them.'

152

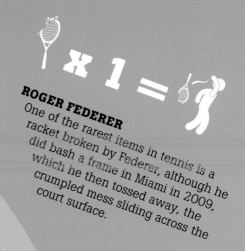

ROGER FEDERER
One of the rarest items in tennis is a racket broken by Federer, although he did bash a frame in Miami in 2009, which he then tossed away, the crumpled mess sliding across the court surface.

NICK KYRGIOS
The Australian has never been one to hold in his emotions. One summer in Cincinnati he sat on his chair during a changeover and broke three rackets in a matter of seconds.

MARCOS BAGHDATIS
One year, over the course of a single changeover at the Australian Open, the Cypriot obliterated four rackets, two still in their wrappers, and so turned himself into a YouTube hit. Serena Williams was astounded: 'I've never done that, that's impressive, wow.'

THE BIG (FAB) FOUR

For the past decade or so, men's tennis has been living through a golden age. Never before had a quartet of players dominated the sport as Roger Federer, Rafael Nadal, Novak Djokovic and Andy Murray have. Their longevity has been extraordinary. Even when all four were in their thirties – or, in Federer's case, the mid-thirties – they maintained their primacy over the rest of the sport.

Davis Cup

All four have won the team competition at least once.

Rankings

Since February 2004, no one outside the Big Four has held the number one ranking (all four players have had their turns at the top).

Olympics

The Big Four have also dominated the past three Olympics, with Nadal scoring the 2008 title in Beijing, while Murray was victorious in London in 2012 and Rio in 2016.

Prize money

The quartet have the four leading positions in the all-time list, with Djokovic the first man in history to reach $100 million, followed by Federer.

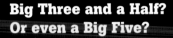

Big Three and a Half?
Or even a Big Five?

For a while, it was said that tennis only had a Big Three and a Half, but that was before Murray won his first Grand Slam at the 2012 US Open and Wimbledon titles in 2013 and 2016. It has also been suggested that Wawrinka's multiple Grand Slams mean we should be talking about a Big Five, but the Swiss himself has said that he has not been consistent enough to be bracketed with the others.

Grand Slams

- A member of the Big Four won the Australian Open every year from 2006 to 2018, apart from 2014, when Stan Wawrinka was the champion.

- Only once from 2005 to 2017 did someone outside the Fab Four of men's tennis win the French Open – when Wawrinka took the title in 2015.

- Every year from 2003 to 2017, one of the four big beasts of men's tennis won Wimbledon.

- The Big Four's run at the US Open has been interrupted just three times between 2004 and 2017 – by Juan Martín del Potro in 2009, by Marin Čilić in 2014 and by Wawrinka in 2016.

ROMANCES

According to a joke that probably originated in an ancient Christmas cracker, you should never date a tennis player. Why so? Because, to them, love means nothing.

Roger Federer and his future wife, Mirka Vavrinec, had their first kiss at the 2000 Sydney Olympics, where they were both competing for Switzerland. They have had four children together – twin girls and twin boys – raising the possibility of the Federers playing the Federers in a Grand Slam mixed doubles final at some point in the future.

Moments after winning a first-round match at a tournament in the Netherlands, **Michaella Krajicek's** German boyfriend, Martin Emmrich, appeared on court. They had met at the same event a year earlier. To begin with, she didn't realise he was about to propose to her. 'The first 10 to 15 seconds when he was on court, I thought, "Oh, it's nice to see him, but this is strange". And then I saw that he had tears in his eyes and I was like, "Oh, wow" and I realised what was going to happen. I was so focused on him the whole time that I didn't hear anything he was saying.' She did, however, say yes.

Caroline Wozniacki and **Rory McIlroy** had already sent out the invitations to their wedding when the golfer called to end the relationship. The conversation lasted little longer than a couple of minutes.

Steffi Graf and Andre Agassi's children – Jaden and Jaz – have the perfect genes for tennis. Graf and Agassi are two of the greatest players to have competed in Grand Slam tennis.

Lleyton Hewitt was once asked how he was helping with preparations for his wedding to Kim Clijsters, to which he said: 'Just going to rock up, mate.' They never made it to the church.

One summer, **Serena Williams** and **Maria Sharapova** had a spectacular and very public falling-out over Grigor Dimitrov, a tennis player they had both dated. In an interview with *Rolling Stone* magazine, Williams spoke of 'the guy with a black heart', so Sharapova retaliated by saying that Williams was having an affair with her married coach, Patrick Mouratoglou.

In the summer of 1974, when they both won a Wimbledon singles title, **Jimmy Connors** and **Chris Evert** were the Love Double or Love Match. As Evert recalls: 'It was a total fairytale. Jimmy and I were two young kids having a good time with no pressure on us, getting a lot of good press. It was a very exciting time for both of us. To win Wimbledon and have alongside you someone you love is almost too good to be true.'

For **Martina Navratilova**, proposing to her girlfriend Julia Lemigova on the big screen in the US Open's Arthur Ashe Stadium made her so nervous it was 'kind of an out-of-body experience'. 'You've seen people propose at sporting events before, in movies and in real life, and there it was happening to me. It was like I was watching myself do it.' Fortunately, Lemigova said yes.

Rats brought **Serena Williams** together with Alexis Ohanian, the founder of Reddit, and the man who would father her child. Williams was in Rome to play a clay-court tournament and she was having a late breakfast with her entourage at her hotel when Ohanian sat down near them. Williams and her group thought Ohanian was too close and tried to encourage him to move away by suggesting there was a rat under his table. Ohanian wasn't bothered: 'I'm from Brooklyn – I see rats all the time.' Amused by his response, Williams invited him to join them. That was in 2015. In 2016, Ohanian proposed to Williams at the same table.

The Serena Slam – four consecutive majors from 2002 to 2003 – might never have happened if **Serena Williams**' heart hadn't been 'torn in half' by an unnamed former boyfriend. 'He left me thinking I was ugly. So I decided that tennis would be my salvation. I would get so-and-so to regret how he had treated me. I wanted him to see me everywhere, to stay in this guy's face, to be a constant reminder of what we had, to rise above his shabby treatment,' said Williams. 'It was all about lifting myself from the dirt he left me lying in.'

SOCIAL MEDIA

Who are the most powerful and influential tennis players on social media? Hookit, an analytics company, looked at the total number of interactions (likes, shares and comments) over 12 months, from June 2015 to June 2016, and also the average number of interactions per post.

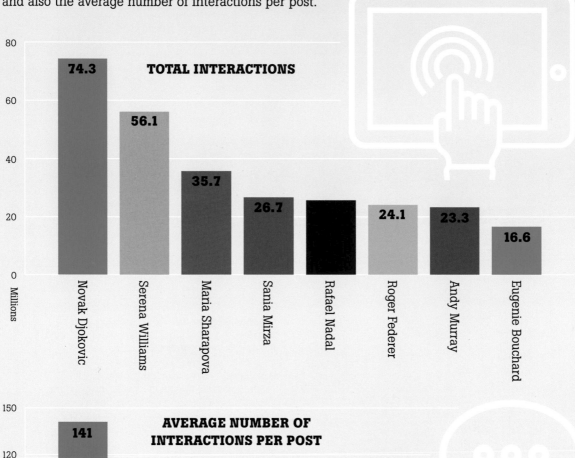

TOTAL INTERACTIONS

Player	Interactions (Millions)
Novak Djokovic	74.3
Serena Williams	56.1
Maria Sharapova	35.7
Sania Mirza	26.7
Rafael Nadal	(26)
Roger Federer	24.1
Andy Murray	23.3
Eugenie Bouchard	16.6

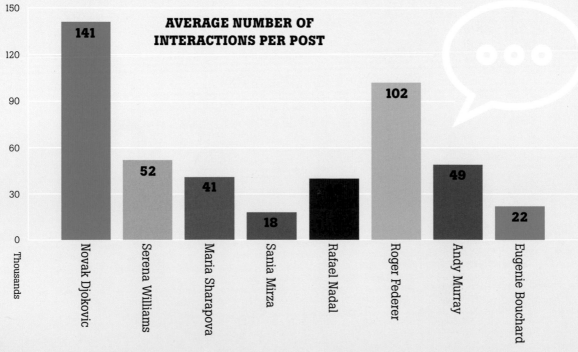

AVERAGE NUMBER OF INTERACTIONS PER POST

Player	Interactions (Thousands)
Novak Djokovic	141
Serena Williams	52
Maria Sharapova	41
Sania Mirza	18
Rafael Nadal	(40)
Roger Federer	102
Andy Murray	49
Eugenie Bouchard	22

SOCIAL MEDIA FOLLOWERS
(PERCENTAGES)

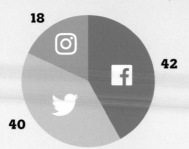

18
42
40

Novak Djokovic

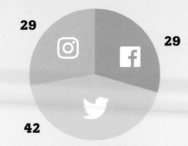

29
29
42

Serena Williams

Instagram

Facebook

Twitter

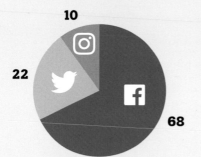

10
22
68

Maria Sharapova

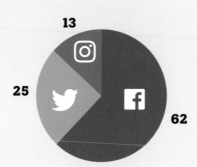

13
25
62

Sania Mirza

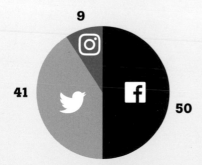

9
41
50

Rafael Nadal

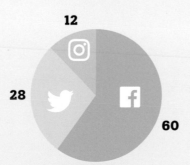

12
28
60

Roger Federer

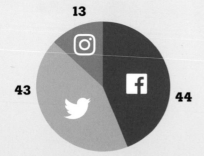

13
43
44

Andy Murray

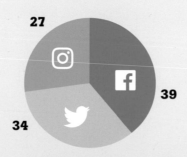

27
34
39

Eugenie Bouchard

ICON MARIA SHARAPOVA

Winning Wimbledon in 2004 at the age of 17 launched Sharapova into the stratosphere, on and off the tennis court. More than just a tennis player, she is also a confectionery entrepreneur with her own range of candy, called Sugarpova.

THE FACTS

NICKNAME
Masha/Shazza

DATE OF BIRTH
19 April 1987

BIRTHPLACE
Nyagan, Russia

HEIGHT
1.88m (6ft 2in)

PLAYING STYLE
Right-handed (two-handed backhand)

15

Sharapova's ban, in months, after she tested positive for meldonium at the 2016 Australian Open. She was initially suspended for two years, but the punishment was reduced after she appealed to the Court of Arbitration for Sport.

RECORDS
10

For more than 10 years in succession, Sharapova was judged by *Forbes* magazine to be the highest-earning female athlete in the world. She has said that she has already earned enough money to feed her great-grandchildren.

SHARAPOVA
IN NUMBERS

130
Sharapova is a Chernobyl survivor. She was in her mother's womb as the radiation cloud from the explosion at the nuclear power station, just 130km (80 miles) away, lingered over eastern Belarus. Amid all the fear and chaos of the Chernobyl fallout zone, Sharapova's parents fled.

700
The amount of money that Sharapova's father, Yuri, had – in US dollars – when he and his nine-year-old daughter arrived in the United States from Russia. To survive, Yuri worked long hours in poorly paid jobs, including sweeping the floor in a grocery store, washing dishes in a restaurant and carrying bricks on a building site.

2
The length of time, in years, that Sharapova didn't see her mother after arriving in the United States. They rarely had the chance to speak on the telephone so communicated via letters.

6
She was only the sixth female player in the Open era to complete the Career Grand Slam.

2013
The year that Sharapova supposedly considered changing her name to Sugarpova to promote her range of candy.

5

Grand Slam titles

Australian Open	French Open	Wimbledon	US Open
1	2	1	1

SPEED AROUND THE COURT AND REACTION TIME

Who are the fastest players? And who are the quickest to react when returning serve? The numbers are according to figures published by Tennis Australia's Game Insight Group.

SPEED AROUND THE COURT

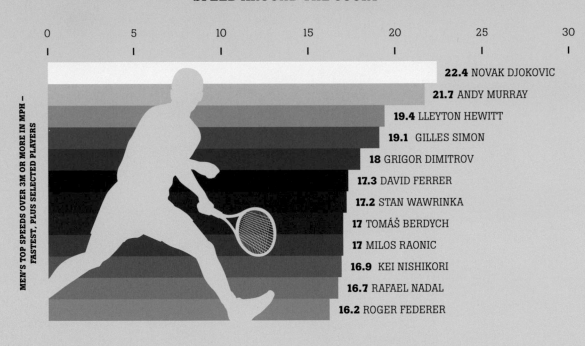

MEN'S TOP SPEEDS OVER 3M OR MORE IN MPH – FASTEST, PLUS SELECTED PLAYERS

22.4	NOVAK DJOKOVIC
21.7	ANDY MURRAY
19.4	LLEYTON HEWITT
19.1	GILLES SIMON
18	GRIGOR DIMITROV
17.3	DAVID FERRER
17.2	STAN WAWRINKA
17	TOMÁŠ BERDYCH
17	MILOS RAONIC
16.9	KEI NISHIKORI
16.7	RAFAEL NADAL
16.2	ROGER FEDERER

WOMEN'S TOP SPEEDS OVER 3M OR MORE IN MPH – FASTEST, PLUS SELECTED PLAYERS

14.3	SIMONA HALEP
14	CARLA SUÁREZ NAVARRO
13.6	DOMINIKA CIBULKOVÁ
13.6	AGNIESZKA RADWAŃSKA
13.6	EUGENIE BOUCHARD
13.5	AJLA TOMLJANOVIĆ
13.3	ANGELIQUE KERBER
13.2	GARBIÑE MUGURUZA
13	ANA IVANOVIĆ
12.9	JULIA GÖERGES
12.8	MARIA SHARAPOVA
12.8	SERENA WILLIAMS
12.1	VICTORIA AZARENKA

REACTION TIME – AVERAGE NUMBER OF SECONDS TO RETURN SERVE

0   0.1   0.2   0.3   0.4   0.5   0.6   0.7   0.8   0.9

MEN'S REACTION TIME – FASTEST, PLUS SELECTED PLAYERS

0.61 NICK KYRGIOS

0.62 ROGER FEDERER

0.64 NOVAK DJOKOVIC

0.64 ANDY MURRAY

0.65 STAN WAWRINKA

0.65 GRIGOR DIMITROV

0.65 KEI NISHIKORI

0.7 MILOS RAONIC

0.71 RAFAEL NADAL

0   0.1   0.2   0.3   0.4   0.5   0.6   0.7   0.8   0.9

WOMEN'S REACTION TIME – FASTEST, PLUS SELECTED PLAYERS

0.67 VENUS WILLIAMS

0.67 CAMILA GIORGI

0.68 ANA IVANOVIĆ

0.68 EUGENIE BOUCHARD

0.68 GARBIÑE MUGURUZA

0.69 SERENA WILLIAMS

0.7 PETRA KVITOVÁ

0.7 VICTORIA AZARENKA

0.71 MARIA SHARAPOVA

0.78 MADISON KEYS

COMEBACKS

Whether they are spectacularly successful, or complete failures, tennis comebacks often make for compelling stories.

**17 GRAND SLAMS
2003–2012**

ROGER FEDERER

**AUSTRALIAN OPEN
2017**

Federer's triumph at the 2017 Australian Open was surely the most improbable comeback in the sport's history (as well as the most popular among tennis fans). The Swiss player hadn't played a tournament for six months, since the previous season's Wimbledon Championships, while recovering from a knee injury he had sustained while running a bath for his children in Melbourne in 2016. Consider also how Federer's opponent in the final was his greatest rival, Rafael Nadal, and how he came from a break down in the final set to score his 18th Grand Slam title, and first for five years.

**13 GRAND SLAMS
1999–2010**

SERENA WILLIAMS

**WIMBLEDON
2012**

Winning Wimbledon is always an emotional experience, and it was especially so for Williams at the 2012 Championships. That was her first Grand Slam after 'being on my death bed at one point, quite literally' following a pulmonary embolism in 2011. 'I can't even describe it. I almost didn't make it a few years. I was in hospital but now I'm here and it was so worth it, I'm so happy.'

COMEBACK 1

MARTINA HINGIS

**COMEBACK 2
DOUBLES PLAYER**

A first comeback was spoilt by testing positive for cocaine at the Wimbledon Championships in 2007. However, after her ban had been served, the Swiss player made a second comeback, this time as a doubles player.

141 RANKING

ANDRE AGASSI

**CAREER GRAND SLAM
1999**

The most distressing year of Agassi's career was 1997, when his ranking spiralled to 141 and he tested positive for crystal meth. Fortunately for Agassi, the ATP accepted his story of unwittingly ingesting the drug after sipping one of his assistant's 'spiked sodas', and just two years later, at the 1999 French Open, he completed the Career Grand Slam.

WINNER ... MONTE CARLO OR BUST

BJÖRN BORG

'It was madness,' Borg has since said of his comeback at the Monte Carlo Country Club in 1991, 10 years on from when he had last been a force in the men's game. Just to make his return even stranger, Borg opted to play with wooden rackets, even though the sport had moved on to graphite frames, and choose as his conditioning coach a Welshman in his late 70s who was a self-proclaimed martial arts and shiatsu expert. Borg lost that match, then all eight he played in 1992 and all three of his appearances in 1993. A dozen defeats in, the comeback was aborted.

8 GRAND SLAMS 1990–1993 AUSTRALIAN OPEN 1996

MONICA SELES

Victory at the 1996 Australian Open was a hugely significant tournament for Seles – that was the only Grand Slam she would win after returning to the tour after being stabbed in Hamburg in 1993.

US OPEN 2005 3 GRAND SLAMS

KIM CLIJSTERS

Motherhood brought out the best in Clijsters during her second tennis career. Before becoming a mum, Clijsters won 'only' one major, a US Open title, but on her return she scored three Grand Slams – two US Open triumphs and one Australian Open title.

1992 OLYMPIC GOLD 3 GRAND SLAMS

JENNIFER CAPRIATI

Capriati's remarkable comeback can be illustrated with two images. The first is the Florida police mugshot taken after her arrest for possession of marijuana and shoplifting. The second is any photograph showing her holding up the 2001 Australian Open title, for what was her first Grand Slam title. A second followed at that year's French Open, and she won a third major at the 2002 Australian Open after saving four match points against Martina Hingis.

18 GRAND SLAM SINGLES TITLES US OPEN MIXED DOUBLES 2006

MARTINA NAVRATILOVA

During her second career on the tour, Martina Navratilova had much success as a doubles player, including winning the 2006 US Open mixed doubles title with Bob Bryan when she was just a month short of her 50th birthday.

SUPERSTITIONS AND RITUALS

From sniffing tennis balls to taking cold showers, tennis players are some of the most superstitious people on this planet.

Rafael Nadal
Nadal can't play unless the labels on his water bottles are facing the side of the court where he is playing. Among many other rituals, Nadal takes a cold shower 45 minutes before a match, always carries one racket in his hand while walking into the stadium, and makes sure he is the last person to approach the net before the coin toss, always keeping his opponent and the umpire waiting.

Serena Williams
The younger Williams sister once admitted to wearing the same unwashed socks during a tournament, even during fortnight-long Grand Slams. She has also confessed to always using the same shower and obsessively taking her shower sandals on court with her, as well as always tying her shoelaces in the same way.

Goran Ivanišević
His victory at the 2001 Wimbledon Championships can't just be attributed to his superstition of watching Teletubbies, a children's TV programme, every morning. There were many other rituals. Every day of the fortnight, he ate the same evening meal of fish soup for starter, a main course of lamb and potatoes, and ice cream with chocolate sauce for dessert – all eaten at the same table of the same restaurant. Just remembering all of his superstitions must have been exhausting – he also had the same breakfast every morning, packed his bag at the same time, and made sure of parking in the same space and using the same shower.

Andre Agassi
The Las Vegan liked to go 'commando' in matches. It was a practice that began at the 1999 French Open when Agassi realised to his horror, in the minutes before he was due on court, that he had forgotten his underwear. His coach, Brad Gilbert, offered to lend him his own, but Agassi declined. Such was the quality of his tennis that day and for the rest of the tournament – he took the title to complete his Career Grand Slam – that Agassi never again wore underpants on court.

Ivan Lendl
You could tell when Lendl was nervous – he would pluck his eyebrows.

Dominika Cibulková
The former Australian Open finalist smells the tennis balls she is about to play with.

Andy Murray
If Murray hits an ace, he will often want the ball back to use for the next point.

Marat Safin
To protect himself from evil spirits and bad karma on the tennis court, the Russian wore an 'evil eye' pendant.

Björn Borg
The Swede's abstinence during Wimbledon – he wouldn't shave or have sex all fortnight – clearly worked: he won five successive titles. Borg's routine included staying in the same room of the same (modest) hotel, always taking the same route to the All England Club, always wearing the same tight, pinstriped shirt and always sitting in the same chair during changeovers.

Andre Agassi
Going without underwear wasn't Agassi's only superstition – he often wouldn't start a point until all the ball kids were in their original positions.

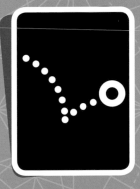

Novak Djokovic
The Serbian doesn't like to use the same shower twice. Previously known for the number of times he bounced the ball before serving – his record was almost 40 bounces – Djokovic has largely found a way to keep that habit under control.

Maria Sharapova and **John McEnroe**
These two tennis stars are among the players who don't like to step on the lines between points.

MOTHERS AND FATHERS

Which players in the Open era have won Grand Slam singles titles after becoming a mother or a father?

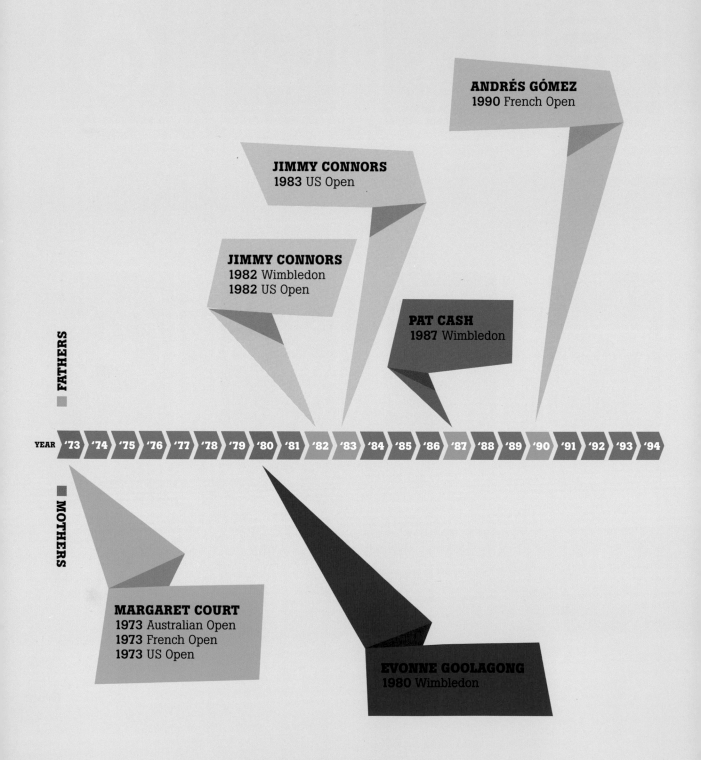

FATHERS

ANDRÉS GÓMEZ
1990 French Open

JIMMY CONNORS
1983 US Open

JIMMY CONNORS
1982 Wimbledon
1982 US Open

PAT CASH
1987 Wimbledon

YEAR '73 '74 '75 '76 '77 '78 '79 '80 '81 '82 '83 '84 '85 '86 '87 '88 '89 '90 '91 '92 '93 '94

MOTHERS

MARGARET COURT
1973 Australian Open
1973 French Open
1973 US Open

EVONNE GOOLAGONG
1980 Wimbledon

NOVAK DJOKOVIC
2015 Wimbledon

NOVAK DJOKOVIC
2015 US Open

NOVAK DJOKOVIC
2016 French Open

ROGER FEDERER
2018 Australian Open

ROGER FEDERER
2017 Wimbledon

BORIS BECKER
1996 Australian Open

NOVAK DJOKOVIC
2016 Australian Open

ROGER FEDERER
2012 Wimbledon

ROGER FEDERER
2017 Australian Open

ANDRE AGASSI
2003 Australian Open

ROGER FEDERER
2010 Australian Open

NOVAK DJOKOVIC
2016 French Open

PETR KORDA
1998 Australian Open

STAN WAWRINKA
2014 Australian Open
All of his Grand Slam
titles have come since
he became a dad.

NOVAK DJOKOVIC
2015 Australian Open

YEVGENY KAFELNIKOV
1999 Australian Open

STAN WAWRINKA
2015 French Open

ALBERT COSTA
2002 French Open

ANDY MURRAY
2016 Wimbledon

STAN WAWRINKA
2016 US Open

'95 '96 '97 '98 '99 '00 '01 '02 '03 '04 '05 '06 '07 '08 '09 '10 '11 '12 '13 '14 '15 '16 '17 '18

KIM CLIJSTERS
2009 US Open

SERENA WILLIAMS
2017 Australian Open
Williams was two
months pregnant with
her first child when
she won the 2017
Australian Open.

KIM CLIJSTERS
2010 US Open

KIM CLIJSTERS
2011 Australian Open

ICON **BORIS BECKER**

From winning Wimbledon at the age of 17 to coaching Novak Djokovic, Becker has been one of the most influential characters in the sport and world of tennis.

THE FACTS

NICKNAME
Boom Boom

DATE OF BIRTH
22 November 1967

BIRTHPLACE
Leimen, former West Germany

HEIGHT
1.90m (6ft 3in)

PLAYING STYLE
Right-handed (one handed backhand)

6

The number of Grand Slam titles won by Novak Djokovic while being coached by Becker.

25

The amount, in millions of US dollars, that Becker won in prize money.

RECORDS

17

Becker's 1985 triumph at Wimbledon – when he was aged just 17 – made him the youngest Wimbledon men's singles champion in history, a record he still holds. It also turned him into public property. 'It was like sitting on the lavatory with the whole world watching,' Becker said.

1

Becker was the first German man to become the world number one. He spent a total of 12 weeks at the top of the rankings.

6

Grand Slam titles

2 **3** **1**

Australian Open   Wimbledon   US Open

BECKER
IN NUMBERS

1

The number of long, black, curly wigs that Becker bought in a Munich fancy-dress shop, which he would wear at the height of his fame. Unfortunately for Becker, he was still occasionally spotted while in disguise, on account of his distinctive walk.

149

The speed, in mph, at which Becker has suggested he was serving when he was 17 years old. This has never been substantiated.

3

The number of times that Becker reached the semi-finals of the French Open, the only Grand Slam that eluded him.

0

The number of titles he won on clay. Becker has said of the surface: 'Clay was difficult because it was against my personality.'

18

Winning Wimbledon at 17 hadn't been a fluke – the following year Becker was the champion once more (but he wouldn't win again at 19).

WHO HIT THE FASTEST SERVES IN TENNIS HISTORY?

Some players' serves have top speeds comparable to those of high-performance sports cars. How long before a male player becomes the first to hit a 170mph serve?

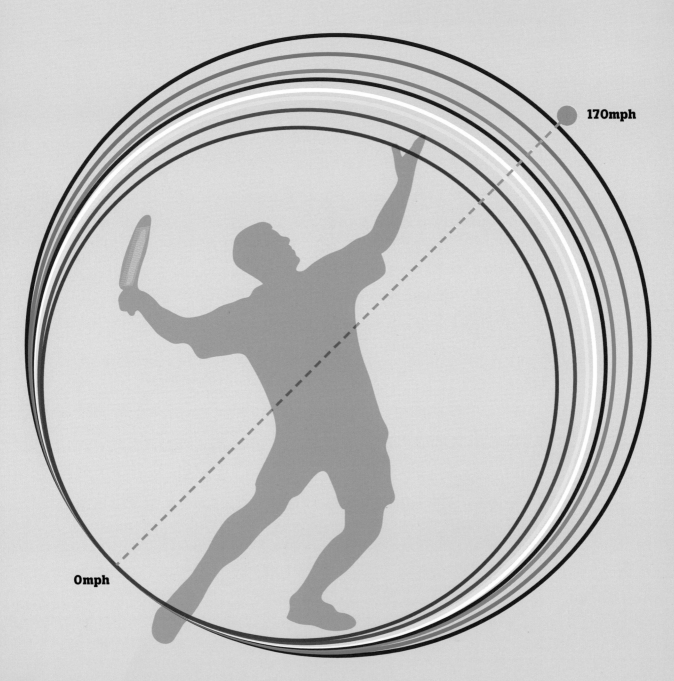

170mph

0mph

Men's leaderboard in mph:

- ▬ 163.7 **Sam Groth** (Australia)
- ▬ 160 **Albano Olivetti** (France)
- ▬ 157 **John Isner** (United States)
- ▬ 156 **Ivo Karlović** (Croatia),
  Jerzy Janowicz (Poland)
- ▬ 155.3 **Milos Raonic** (Canada)
- ▬ 155 **Andy Roddick** (United States)
- ▬ 153 **Roscoe Tanner** (United States)
- ▬ 152 **Joachim Johansson** (Sweden),
  Feliciano López (Spain)

Women's leaderboard in mph:

- ▬ 131 **Sabine Lisicki** (Germany)
- ▬ 129 **Venus Williams** (United States),
  Serena Williams (United States)
- ▬ 126 **Julia Göerges** (Germany),
  Caroline Garcia (France),
  Brenda Schultz-McCarthy
  (Netherlands)
- ▬ 125.5 **Nadiya Kichenok** (Ukraine)
- ▬ 125 **Anna-Lena Groenefeld** (Germany),
  Lucie Hradecká (Czech Republic),
  Ana Ivanovic (Serbia),
  Denisa Allertová (Czech Republic)
- ▬ 124 **Kristina Mladenovic** (France)

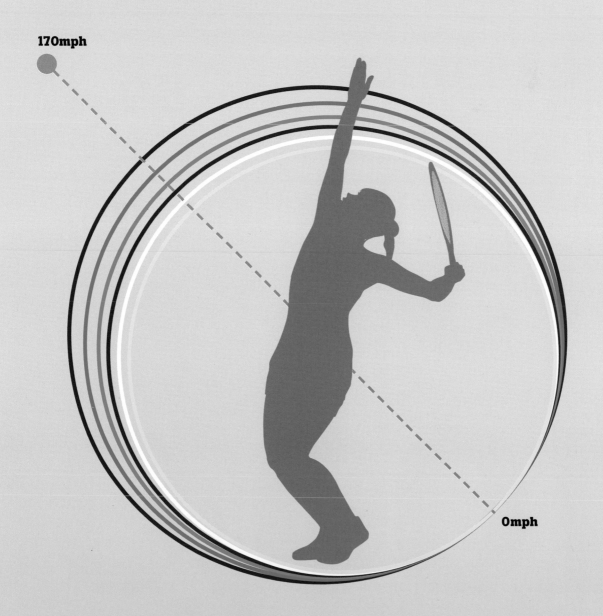

170mph

0mph

THE US OPEN IN NUMBERS

Each of the four Grand Slams has taken on some of the characteristics of the city in which it is played, but none more so than the US Open, which displays much of the noise, energy and emotion of New York.

7.5
The weight, in tonnes, of crab, shrimp and lobster sold each year.

225,000
The number of burgers and hotdogs sold at the tournament each year (no wonder this is the only major where players on the outside courts can smell burgers frying).

50 million
The 2017 US Open was the first Grand Slam with a prize money pot in excess of US$50 million.

3.7 million
The amount, in US dollars, that was paid to each of the singles champions at the 2017 US Open.

57
The percentage of spectators who are female.

Approximate annual revenue, in US dollars, from ticket sales.

100,00

2017

For the first time since 1981, four American players reached the women's singles semi-finals.

3

The US Open is the only one of the four Grand Slams to have been played on three different surfaces. A grass-court event from 1881 to 1974, it had three brief years as a clay-court tournament, before switching to hard courts in 1978, a surface it has stuck with.

20

The length of the interruption, in minutes, during a second-round match between John McEnroe and Ilie Nastase at the 1979 Open, during which spectators tossed beer cans and other debris onto the court. Fearing a riot, the police moved onto the playing surface. The reason for the disturbance was that Nastase had been defaulted for protesting at McEnroe's slow play. In the end, Nastase was reinstated and the umpire was changed – and McEnroe won the restarted match.

160,000

The average household income of spectators, in US dollars.

0,000

BY THE NUMBERS
TENNIS BETTING

Tennis has grown into a popular sport for gamblers, a development that has brought suspicion and scandals. From bribes to match-fixing bans, the stakes are high.

7 MILLION

The amount of money, in US dollars, that was gambled on a match between Russia's Nikolay Davydenko and Argentina's Martin Vassallo Argüello at a tournament in Sopot, Poland, in 2007. Davydenko retired through injury in the third set. Citing irregular betting patterns, Betfair, a peer-to-peer gaming exchange, voided all wagers. The ATP later investigated the circumstances surrounding the match and found no evidence to suggest that Davydenko was involved in match-fixing or corruption.

5 BILLION

The estimated size, in US dollars, of the global tennis betting market.

2

Tennis is the second-biggest sport for the betting industry in the United Kingdom, only trailing football.

2011

The year that an Austrian, Daniel Koellerer, became the first player to be banned for life for match-fixing.

100,000

The estimated bribe, in US dollars, for throwing a match on the men's or women's tour.

200,000

The amount of money, in US dollars, that Novak Djokovic was once offered to throw a match at a tournament in Russia. The offer was made indirectly, and he didn't entertain the thought or even end up playing at the tournament.

292

The number of matches in 2016 for which the Tennis Integrity Unit received an alert over suspicious betting patterns, out of 114,126 professional matches played that year. That was up from 246 alerts the season before.

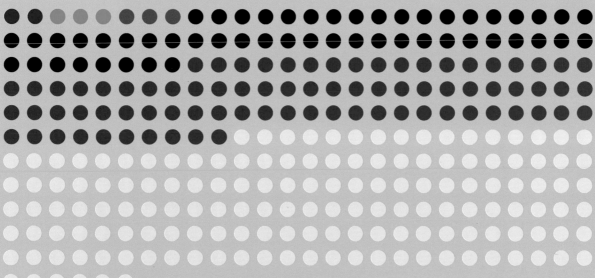

- **2** — ATP (men's tour)
- **3** — Grand Slams
- **3** — WTA (women's tour)
- **52** — ITF Women's Futures (lowest level of women's professional tennis)
- **80** — ATP Challenger (one level below men's main tour)
- **152** — ITF Men's Futures (lowest level of men's professional tennis)

DEFAULTS

Tennis isn't always such a civilised sport – some players have behaved so badly that they have received point penalties or even been defaulted from matches.

MATCH DEFAULT

Stefan Koubek was defaulted from the 2000 French Open after throwing his racket, which struck a ball kid.

Tim Henman became the first player to be defaulted from Wimbledon in the Open era when he smashed a ball away in anger during a doubles match in 1995 and accidentally hit a ball girl. He apologised the next day with flowers and a kiss.

A French umpire needed surgery to repair a fractured eye socket after being hit by a tennis ball angrily belted away by Canada's **Denis Shapovalov** during a Davis Cup tie against Great Britain in Ottawa in 2017. The teenager, who hadn't meant to strike the official, was defaulted from the fifth rubber, giving the British team a 3–2 victory.

x!!@!!

Only once in **John McEnroe's** career was he defaulted. That unhappy incident occurred during a fourth-round match at the 1990 Australian Open when, having earlier intimidated an official and smashed a racket, the New Yorker swore at a supervisor.

x!!x!!

Hitting a ball into the stands, and being 'verbally abusive' towards the umpire, saw **Andre Agassi** defaulted from a tournament in Indianapolis in 1996. If Agassi was furious, he wasn't half as upset as the crowd, who threw towels, paper and water bottles on to the court.

POINT DEFAULT

Exhibition matches are supposed to be friendly, even light-hearted, occasions, but that message didn't appear to have reached **John McEnroe** and **Jimmy Connors** when they played one in 1982. The point penalties awarded that day hardly restrained the pair of them, who very nearly punched each other.

You cannot be serious!

At match point down against Kim Clijsters in the semi-finals of the 2009 US Open, **Serena Williams** raged at a lineswoman who had called her for a foot-fault, threatening her with a tennis ball. With Williams receiving a point penalty for her language and intimidating behaviour, the match was over.

'The devils were crawling all over my brain that afternoon,' **John McEnroe** has recalled of his first-round match at the 1981 Wimbledon Championships. McEnroe's anger at the umpire Ted James produced two of the most famous quotes in tennis history. The first was: 'You cannot be serious!' The second was when the New Yorker called James 'the absolute pits of the world'. James, mishearing 'pits', said to the player: 'I'm going to award a point against you because you're so rude.' McEnroe's behaviour later generated another point penalty, which was for swearing at the tournament referee.

PARENTAL ADVISORY: EXPLICIT CONTENT

OFF COURT

Controversial behaviour isn't limited to those on court. Lip-readers spotted Andy Murray's future wife **Kim Sears** using some colourful language during her husband's semi-final against Tomas Berdych at the 2015 Australian Open. She appeared for the final wearing a T-shirt that declared: 'Parental Advisory: Explicit Content.'

COMMERCIAL BREAKS

Tennis players are often enticed to endorse brands and products. Here are some of the most memorable campaigns and photo shoots.

'Only the ball should bounce,' Anna Kournikova declared from a thousand billboards in an advertising campaign for Berlei sports bras.

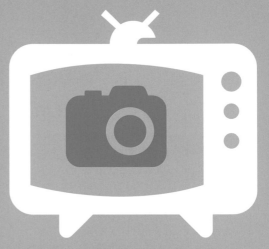

'Image is everything,' Andre Agassi said in an advert for Canon cameras. 'Overnight, the slogan became synonymous with me. Sportswriters liken this slogan to my inner nature, my essential being. They say it's my philosophy, my religion, and they predict it's going to be my epitaph,' Agassi wrote in his autobiography, *Open*.

Eugenie Bouchard, Caroline Wozniacki and Serena Williams have all appeared in the *Sports Illustrated Swimsuit* issue.

In a television commercial for Armani, Rafael Nadal runs through a car park in a tuxedo, taking his clothes off as he moves.

A couple of female airport security staff threatened to strip-search Roger Federer in an advertisement for Lindt chocolates.

Real or fake? There was some debate about the veracity of footage that supposedly showed Federer goofing around on the set of a shoot for Gillette razors. Did Federer really hit a serve that knocked a bottle of water off an assistant's head?

'Nike is McEnroe's favourite four-letter word' was the slogan that played on John McEnroe's status as the angriest man in tennis.

Novak Djokovic once played tennis while standing on the wings of a flying biplane. Or at least his racket sponsor, Head, produced a film that appeared to show the Serbian doing just that.

GREATEST MATCHES

Sometimes watching tennis becomes so fraught and tense that you can hardly look, and you end up watching the action through your fingers or from behind the sofa.

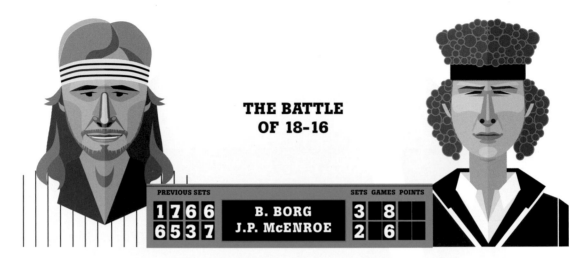

THE BATTLE OF 18-16

PREVIOUS SETS					SETS	GAMES	POINTS		
1	7	6	6	B. BORG	3	8			
6	5	3	7	J.P. McENROE	2	6			

You're not a true tennis fan until you've watched the fourth-set tiebreak of the men's **1980 Wimbledon final** at least half a dozen times. Even now, when you already know the result, you can still feel the tension as John McEnroe saved Björn Borg's five match points before taking the tie-break 18–16. It looked as though McEnroe had the momentum he needed, but Borg steadied himself and won the final set to score a fifth successive Wimbledon title.

PREVIOUS SETS					SETS	GAMES	POINTS		
5	6	6	6	N. DJOKOVIC	3	7			
7	4	2	7	R. NADAL	2	5			

TRULY EPIC
'Epic' is a word used too casually in tennis. Too often, a long tennis match is described as such, when the reality is that very few contests deserve the description. However, Novak Djokovic's victory over Rafael Nadal in the **2012 Australian Open final** – which lasted almost six hours – truly deserved the e-word.

PREVIOUS SETS					SETS	GAMES	POINTS		
5	7	7	3	R. FEDERER	3	16			
7	6	6	6	A. RODDICK	2	14			

GOING THE DISTANCE
The deeper the **2009 Wimbledon final** went into the fifth set, the greater the concern that Roger Federer's heavily pregnant wife, Mirka, would start her contractions. In the end, Federer fended off Andy Roddick to take the fifth set 16–14, and so became the most successful man in tennis history, with victory bringing up his 15th Grand Slam title. The twins arrived later that summer.

PREVIOUS SETS					SETS	GAMES	POINTS
6	7	7	7	P. SAMPRAS	3		
7	6	6	6	A. AGASSI	1		

SHOOT-OUT SETS

Adrenalin levels were spiking in New York City when Pete Sampras played Andre Agassi in the quarter-final of the **2001 US Open**. Sampras won in four sets, all of which were tie-breaks.

PREVIOUS SETS				SETS	GAMES	POINTS
4	7	9	V. WILLIAMS	2		
6	6	7	L. DAVENPORT	1		

KEEPING YOUR NERVE

Saving a match point in a Wimbledon final takes some nerve. Venus Williams did just that in beating Lindsay Davenport for the **2005 title**, winning the third set 9–7 in a match that took almost three hours.

PREVIOUS SETS		SETS	GAMES	POINTS
6	6	V. WILLIAMS	2		
2	4	S. WILLIAMS	0		

SISTER ACT

History was made at the **2001 US Open**, which brought the first Grand Slam final between two sisters since Maud Watson beat Lillian for the 1884 Wimbledon title, 117 years before. Back to the 21st century, and Venus Williams beat Serena in straight sets.

PREVIOUS SETS			SETS	GAMES	POINTS
4	7	6	J. CAPRIATI	2		
6	6	2	M. HINGIS	1		

BOILING OVER

In the boiling Melbourne sunshine – these were conditions that would have melted most players' resolve – Jennifer Capriati was at her most resilient in the **2002 Australian Open final**. Having trailed by a set and 0–4, she staved off four match points to defeat Martina Hingis.

NIGHT VISION

	21.16	MATCH END TIME	MATCH DURATION	4.48	

PREVIOUS SETS					SETS	GAMES	POINTS
4	4	7	7	R. FEDERER	2	7	
6	6	6	6	R. NADAL	3	9	

It was the evening when the Centre Court crowd learned that Roger Federer, who had won the previous five Wimbledons, did indeed have a weakness at the All England Club – a lack of night vision. The **2008 men's singles final**, won by Rafael Nadal, is widely regarded as the greatest tennis match of all time, and for those watching at home, the tennis could be enjoyed in all its glory, thanks to the television director brightening the picture. For the players, though, it wasn't always easy to make out the ball in the near-darkness. Federer's domination of the tournament ended at 9.16p.m. that night, with Nadal scoring his first title.

GREATEST RIVALRIES
BY THE NUMBERS

Great rivalries have brought tennis to life over the years – but who has had the better of those match-ups? And which supposed rivalry, between two of the greats of the modern game, is actually so lopsided as to be a non-rivalry?

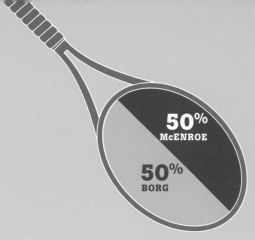

50%
McENROE

50%
BORG

Björn Borg
vs
John McEnroe
14 matches played

46%
EVERT

54%
NAVRATTILOVA

Chris Evert
vs
Martina Navratilova
80 matches played

33%
SELES

67%
GRAF

Steffi Graf
vs
Monica Seles
15 matches played

Rafael Nadal
vs
Roger Federer

Novak Djokovic
vs
Rafael Nadal

Roger Federer
vs
Novak Djokovic

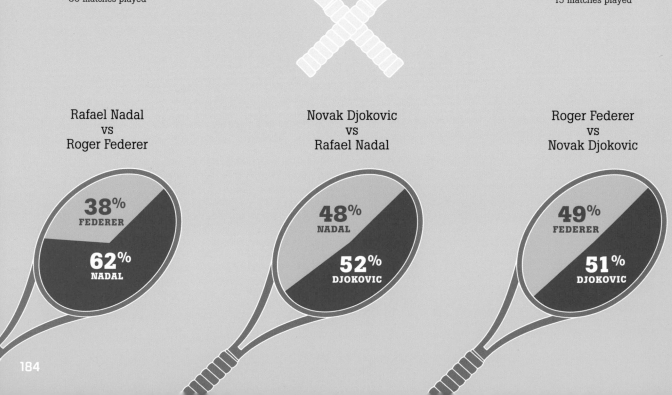

38%
FEDERER

62%
NADAL

48%
NADAL

52%
DJOKOVIC

49%
FEDERER

51%
DJOKOVIC

58% LENDL

42% McENROE

Ivan Lendl
vs
John McEnroe
36 matches played

59% McENROE

41% CONNORS

John McEnroe
vs
Jimmy Connors
34 matches played

59% SAMPRAS

41% AGASSI

Pete Sampras
vs
Andre Agassi
34 matches played

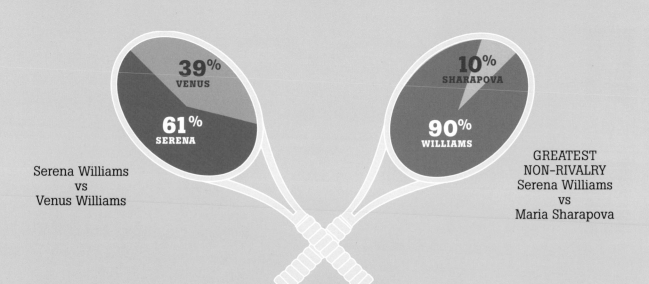

39% VENUS

61% SERENA

Serena Williams
vs
Venus Williams

10% SHARAPOVA

90% WILLIAMS

GREATEST
NON-RIVALRY
Serena Williams
vs
Maria Sharapova

Andy Murray
vs
Roger Federer

Andy Murray
vs
Rafael Nadal

Andy Murray
vs
Novak Djokovic

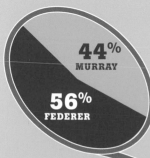

44% MURRAY

56% FEDERER

29% MURRAY

71% NADAL

31% MURRAY

69% DJOKOVIC

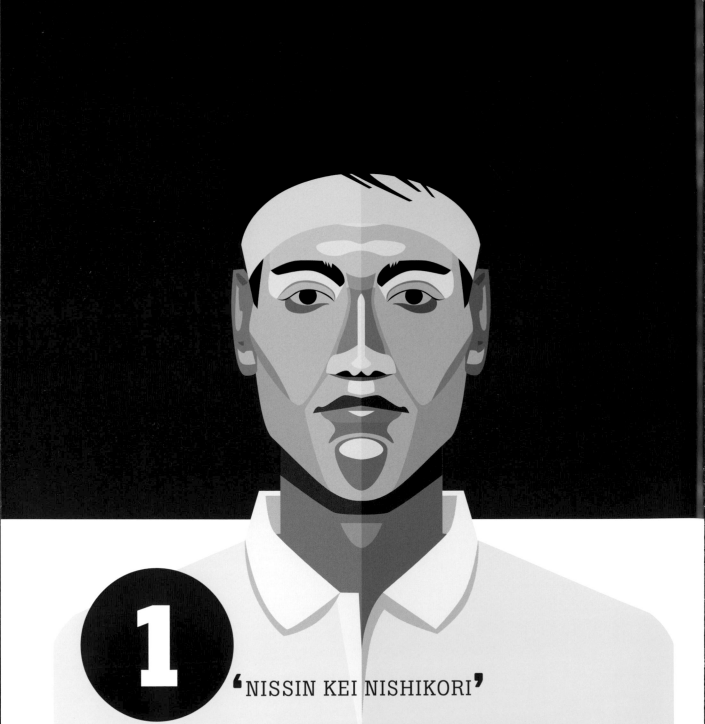

1

'NISSIN KEI NISHIKORI'

The first tennis player to add a sponsor to his name, after he agreed
a deal with a noodle brand, Nissin. The media are supposed to
address him as 'Nissin Kei Nishikori'.

NISHIKORI

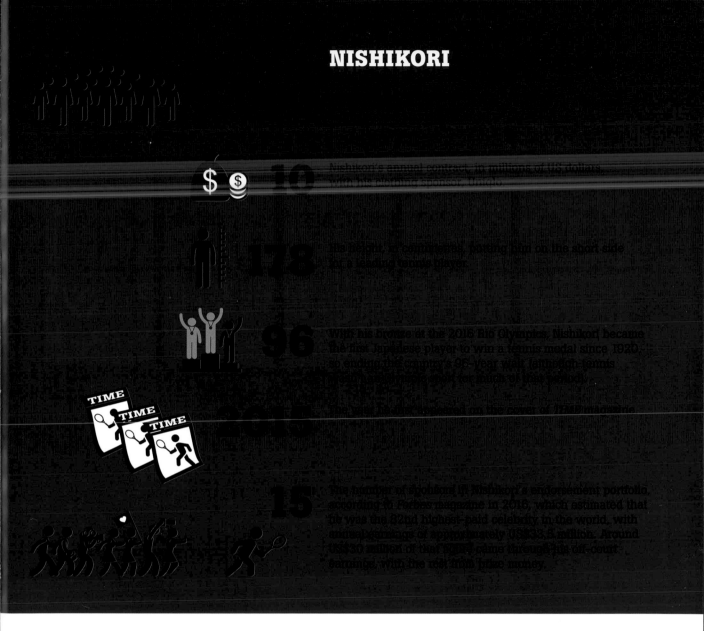

$ 10 — Nishikori's annual contract, in millions of US dollars, with his clothing sponsor, Uniqlo.

178 — His height, in centimeters, putting him on the short side for a leading tennis player.

96 — With his bronze at the 2016 Rio Olympics, Nishikori became the first Japanese player to win a tennis medal since 1920, so ending the country's 96-year wait. (singles tennis was not an Olympic sport for much of that period)

2016 — the year he first appeared on the cover of *TIME* magazine.

15 — The number of sponsors in Nishikori's endorsement portfolio, according to *Forbes* magazine in 2016, which estimated that he was the 32nd highest-paid celebrity in the world, with annual earnings of approximately US$33.5 million. Around US$30 million of that total came through his off-court earnings, with the rest from prize money.

1

The first Japanese player to have a top 10 singles ranking.

1

The first Asian man to appear in a Grand Slam singles final with his run at the 2014 US Open, where he was the runner-up to Croatia's Marin Čilić.

LOSING STREAKS AND QUICK DEFEATS

Success breeds success – and failure can breed failure. Here are some of the longest, and most memorable, losing streaks – and embarrassing results.

Vince Spadea

Once described as 'the Charlie Brown of tennis', Spadea lost 21 consecutive matches, an Open-era record for men's tennis. The American's streak ended with a first-round victory over Greg Rusedski at Wimbledon in 2000, which resulted in the British newspaper headline: 'Rusedski falls to world's biggest loser.'

Arantxa Rus

When the Dutch player lost in the opening round of the 2013 Wimbledon Championships, it extended her losing streak to 17 consecutive matches, which tied the record for women's tennis. The only other woman to have lost 17 straight matches at WTA level was Sandy Collins, from the United States, in the 1980s.

Yevgeny Kafelnikov

Unfortunately for the Russian, and for tennis as a whole, Kafelnikov became world number one in 1999 in curious circumstances – having just lost his opening match at six consecutive tournaments.

Vitas Gerulaitis

'Nobody beats Vitas Gerulaitis 17 times in a row.' So said Gerulaitis himself after victory over Jimmy Connors ended a run of 16 defeats against that opponent.

Maria Sharapova

The Russian's defeat to Serena Williams at the 2016 Australian Open took Sharapova's run of consecutive defeats against the American to 18.

Thierry Champion

Five men have experienced the indignity of a 6–0, 6–0, 6–0 defeat, otherwise known as a 'triple bagel', at a Grand Slam tournament. The last man to be force-fed three bagels was Thierry Champion, when playing Sergi Bruguera in the second round at the French Open in 1993.

Bernard Tomic

The shortest-ever completed match in ATP history was Bernard Tomic's defeat to Jarkko Nieminen in Miami in 2014, which lasted a mere 28 minutes.

Marion Boundy

The shortest ever completed professional match in history was Marion Boundy's defeat to Susan Tutt at the 1969 Wimbledon Championships, which took just 20 minutes.

Natasha Zvereva

A big, fat zero – that's the number of games that Zvereva won against Steffi Graf in the 1988 French Open final, which lasted 32 minutes.

A LIFE AFTER TENNIS

What do tennis players do in retirement? Some turn to religion, crime or politics, others to business or espionage.

ANDREA JAEGER

Jaeger, a former world number two, turned to religion in retirement, becoming Sister Andrea. 'Pretty radical' as her friend, former supermodel Cindy Crawford, put it. Jaeger has said: 'It's a strict discipline. I wake at 4am, do my prayers and my spiritual study, then I start work around 5am or 6am. How often I wear nun's habits depends on what I'm doing. I keep getting the robes stuck in buses and escalators. Once I jumped in a cab and left half of it outside the door. The first time I wore one … a bird went to the bathroom on me. I thought that was God's way of saying, "maybe it's okay to be a little muddy on the edges – you're the one who used to dive for balls on the tennis court".'

ALICE MARBLE

How many other former Wimbledon and US Open champions have been shot in the back and left for dead while operating as a wartime spy? Marble's tennis career was exciting enough, but it had nothing on the drama of her retirement. After the death of her husband, and her own attempted suicide, she accepted a request from US intelligence to spy on a former lover, a Swiss banker, who was helping Nazi Germany to hide the gold, art and other materials looted in occupied Europe. Unfortunately, the Russians had infiltrated the mission and a double agent shot Marble. Miraculously, she survived, and some of her intelligence was used at the Nuremberg Trials.

ROSCOE TANNER

Buying a 32-foot yacht with a dud cheque and then using the boat to obtain a loan landed Tanner in German and American prisons. Since retiring, he has been arrested numerous times, for, among other things, passing off bad cheques, failing to pay child support and not turning up to court.

MARAT SAFIN

'The best-looking guy in the Duma, but that's only because all the other guys are older than 60' – Safin's own assessment after he was elected to a seat in the lower house of the Russian Federal Assembly.

ION TIRIAC

Former French Open quarter-finalist Tiriac is the first retired player to make it onto the *Forbes* billionaires list. The Romanian – who also coached, mentored and managed Boris Becker, Ilie Nastase, Guillermo Vilas, Marat Safin and Goran Ivanišević – has owned his own bank and airline.

ARTHUR ASHE

In his playing days Ashe was the most thoughtful of champions, and in retirement he continued to voice his opinions through his new roles: author and civil rights activist. He wrote 'A Hard Road to Glory', a history of black athletes in America, and was arrested during an anti-apartheid rally outside the South African embassy in Washington.

GABRIELA SABATINI

The US Open champion is said to have earned tens of millions of dollars from her range of perfumes.

For Amy, Molly and Rosie.

ACKNOWLEDGEMENTS

Many thanks to editors Lucy Warburton, Emma Harverson and
Ru Merritt at Quarto for their enthusiasm and direction during this
project. Designers Nick Clark and Paul Oakley have done a fantastic job
at illustrating my ideas. I'm also grateful to copyeditor John Andrews
and proofreader Anna Southgate, and to James Buddell for casting an
eye over the pages. Also thanks to my agent David Luxton.

IMAGE CREDITS

Shutterstock (VAZZEN) 9, (Alhovik) 16, 17, 90 (MiodragF) 16, 17, 72, 73,
81, (knahthra) 22, (browndogstudios) 26, 187 (nnnae) 26, (VoodooDot)
26, (z-Art) 26, (Ansty) 27 , (Leremy) 27, 32, 33, 54, 55, 70, 178,
(Ysami) 27, (Emir Simsek) 39, (DR Travel Photo and Video) 58, 59, 131,
(Bojanovic) 72, 73, 94, (nemlaza) 72, 73, 90, 91 (Snap2Art) 73, (antpkr)
89, (Bokica) 95, (cupoftea) 120, (Real Illusion) 120, 121, (AKV) 121,
(sunlight77) 121, (Lole) 122, (kontur-vid) 142, (Jethita) 182, 183.
Illustrated portraits © Paul Oakley
Various symbols and icons adapted from artworks supplied by
The Noun Project (thenounproject.com).
All other images illustrated by Nick Clark, Jane McKenna and
Paul Oakley.

DATA SOURCES

Every effort has been made to verify the accuracy of data up to the
end of December 2017, unless otherwise stated. Some statistics will
inevitably change over time, but the publishers will be glad to rectify
in future editions any omissions brought in writing to their attention.
Some statistics will change quicker than others. Please refer to the
credited sources below and as stated on relevant pages for latest
information.
Official IBM data 29, 90-91; official data from the ATP World Tour
94-95, 172-173; official data from WTA 172-173

First published in 2018 by Aurum Press,
an imprint of The Quarto Group
The Old Brewery
6 Blundell Street
London N7 9BH
United Kingdom
www.QuartoKnows.com

ISBN 978-1-78131-694-8

10 9 8 7 6 5 4 3 2 1
2022 2021 2020 2019 2018

Design: www.fogdog.co.uk
Illustrated portraits: Paul Oakley
Infographic illustration: Nick Clark,
Jane McKenna, Paul Oakley

Printed in China

Brimming with creative inspiration, how-to projects and useful
information to enrich your everyday life, Quarto Knows is a favourite
destination for those pursuing their interests and passions. Visit our
site and dig deeper with our books into your area of interest: Quarto
Creates, Quarto Cooks, Quarto Homes, Quarto Lives, Quarto Drives,
Quarto Explores, Quarto Gifts, or Quarto Kids.